LOVE
THE BEAT GOES ON

LYNDA FILLER

TABLE OF CONTENTS

Thank you, Dr. Wayne W. Dyer
It's so appropriate that a woman who believes in active dreaming
should receive your message while in that semi-awake state.
If you hadn't asked the question, I might not be able to say:
"Yes. I'm ready to tell my story now."

For

Félix

In August of 2015, Dr. Wayne M. Dyer passed away. He was a mentor to millions, a leading inspiration in the self-help field, and a staunch believer that our biography creates our biology. I've read many of his forty books and listened to countless lectures and interviews. I feel like I know him, and when he passed, it was like losing a close friend.

A few days after Dr. Dyer died, I was sleeping peacefully when a very loud, yet familiar, voice said to me, "Are you ready yet?"

I sat straight up in bed and laughed out loud.

In 2008, I was told that my heart was not responding to the medication prescribed for an extremely serious medical condition. The cardiologist told me to get my affairs in order. In doctor-speak, that means "*Get ready to die!*"

It's now 2017, and I love that my beat goes on. My amazing, beautiful heart is normal, and recent changes in my life are allowing me to live a life I created on my vision board. The number one thing on that board was to write out my personal journey of healing.

If there's even one word or action I've taken that inspires you or makes a difference in your health — no matter what your issues are — then I've fulfilled my life's purpose.

I know you're reading this from the "other side," Dr. Dyer. I wasn't ready to share my story then, but I'm ready now!

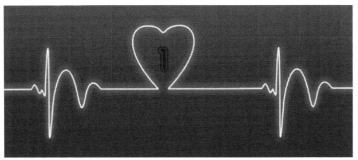

THE WIDOW MAKER

Early in 2008, every website I turned to insisted Dilated Cardiomyopathy can't be healed.

Even now, in 2017, many medical sites still concur. According to the majority of medical doctors, there are many "dis-eases" that cannot be healed. This is simply one of them.

It's been ten years since I was diagnosed. Most websites in 2008 told us life expectancy with this illness was a maximum of five years. I proved to myself that the medical profession (and the internet) doesn't have all the answers.

In all fairness to the specialists in the world, they are simply overwhelmed with "dis-ease." They do an amazing job of fixing our machines using the knowledge, drugs and equipment they have, but they don't have the time in a normal visit to go into the emotional aspects of healing ourselves.

Emotions can be messy and uncomfortable and play such an important part in our health or in the healing process, so I refer to all illness as "dis-ease."

My three-minute YouTube video series tell the story in short bursts of ideas, encouragement and love. Many of you have written and asked me to tell you what I did. To do that, first I need to tell you the aspects of my life that led to who I am. Again, **I'm not a medical doctor:** *my words will never replace whatever your cardiologist or specialist is telling you to do.* Take the medications, take your doctors' advice, but do what I'm about to share with you too.

Heart disease is still the number one killer in the United States today. About every twenty-five seconds, an American will have a coronary event, and one person every minute will die from some of these events. It was once thought of as a "man's disease," and was referred to as the "Widow Maker." It's now the number one killer and dis-abler of *both* men and women in the United States.

Heart disease is only one of many illnesses that are killing us prematurely. But how much of the damage being done is actually related to what goes on in the mind, which is then manifested into our bodies?

There are many studies being done on that very subject, but many of you found me on YouTube and Facebook, and you don't want to wait for those studies…you want answers *now*!

We all know there are common sense-things that need to be done — lose weight, stop smoking, drink less or not at all, and exercise more. Those are a given for optimal health no matter what's going on with your physical body. But what about the emotional work needed to fix the mess that contributed to our broken hearts/broken bodies in the first place?

That's the part of my journey I'm about to share with you.

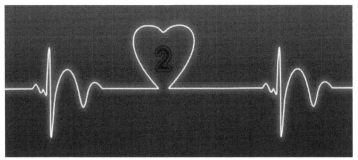

THE BEAT GOES ON

When I look back on it, I realize my health issue had started long before I was diagnosed in early 2008.

In the late nineties, while living in Whistler, British Columbia, I was having a routine check-up for something at the clinic, when the nurse said, "Let's do an EKG."

She was not pleased with the results and insisted I make an appointment with a renowned cardiologist at the University of British Columbia.

If you're unfamiliar with the Canadian Health Care system, now's the time to let you know the doctors are great, but the system is flawed. Just getting an appointment with a specialist can take months…unless you've actually just had a heart attack, then it might *only* take two weeks! The price is right, but the patient could die waiting for care.

My appointment with the specialist was in the spring — possibly in 1998, if I recall correctly — a few months after the EKG. The doctor did his check-up and put me on some type of machine for a stress test.

Now, I know all about stress. I could have told him, without the test, that my life is *filled* with stress — work, personal relationship, and the general disappointments of my life. Not a lot different than most peoples' lives.

The cardiologist told me I was in great shape for a seventy year old…but I was only *fifty*!

He wanted a follow-up appointment, and of course, it was months out. So I completely forgot about it. It was probably in November, which is vacation time for those who work in the ski industry. In any case, I was feeling fine, so I went to Mexico on vacation.

This is one of the leading problems with women and their health — *neglect*. We tend to neglect ourselves in all aspects of our lives, sometimes until it's too late.

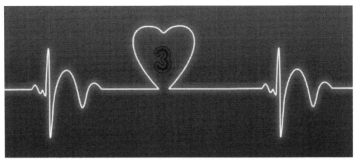

HURRICANES AND OTHER LIFE-ALTERING EVENTS

In October of 2002, I was comfortably sleeping in bed on the ninth floor of the Sheraton Buganvillia Hotel, when I felt the bed begin to shake. It was eight-thirty in the morning, and I got up, looked out the window of my oceanfront condominium…and was shocked at what I saw.

The usual soft, sun-kissed, misty morning over the Bay of Banderas, had been replaced by wave after wave of murky, turbulent, *humongous* blasts of water. Everything appeared monotone grey. The winds howled and pounded the shore, dragging the sand outward and eliminating the beach. The palm trees were bowing down, almost to the breaking point.

Hurricane Kenna had just hit Puerto Vallarta, Mexico. I was mesmerized. Instead of retreating, packing, and taking the stairs down to the main floor, I grabbed my Nikon and started shooting.

I take total responsibility for that hurricane. Let me tell you why…

Puerto Vallarta is in a hurricane zone, like most of the Eastern and Western coastlines of Mexico, but Puerto Vallarta is built around the magnificent deep Banderas Bay and is protected by the surrounding Sierra Madre Mountains. In the last sixty years, there's only been one hurricane.

That's right. *My* hurricane.

I have a friend, Cheryl, who was on a work contract in Sandestin, Florida. The Florida Panhandle…now *that's* a hurricane area! Every year, the communities prepare and discuss what the hurricane season is predicted to be like — whether it will be major, minor or not at all.

I was in my office in Whistler, B. C. the month before my trip to Puerto Vallarta when Cheryl called.

"So what's new?" I asked.

"We're having hurricane warnings. It's exciting!"

"*What!* Are you crazy, Cheryl?"

"No. Listen. I'm sticking my phone out the patio door!" I could suddenly hear the intense roar of the winds. "That's insane. Isn't it dangerous?"

"Nah, the locals are used to it. Every year, around this time, the winds get fierce. They roll in over the Gulf of Mexico. The sky's amazing, all bruised and dangerous, but beautiful."

"You are so lucky to experience something like that! I'd be out there with my camera. Be safe my friend." I ended the call, then thought to myself, *One day, I want to experience a hurricane!*

Remember that old expression *Be careful what you wish for*? I have an amazing ability to manifest things in my life. I've found it most effective for parking spaces in busy areas. But hurricanes, now that's taking it to extremes.

Hurricane Kenna 2002 was the day I decided to resign from my high-stress career in British Columbia, leave my disastrous marriage, and move to Mexico.

I like *big* messages, and this was one of the biggest!

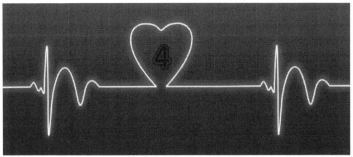

DR. LYNDA

After Hurricane Kenna in 2002, I decided I'd had enough of the life I was living. It's a long story — more than I want to tell here and now and this book is not meant to be a memoir of my entire life — but I took my "big message" and left behind what some would call an amazing career, a multi-million dollar home I had designed and helped build with an incredible contractor, and a husband who was not surprised that I was leaving. My kids were at the age where they were on their own paths.

I loved my life in the early 2000's. Mexico is an amazing place to be for a "free spirit," something I'd forgotten existed inside me. I discovered living without the day-to-day challenges of managing thirty - forty people to be liberating. I no longer had an unsatisfactory relationship, and I found someone new to love — however inappropriate it might've appeared to those wanting stability and a future. I explored a freedom I'd forgotten I could have.

In *Target in the Sun,* my first novel, I wrote about some the exploits I witnessed, and firsthand accounts of life in Puerto Vallarta. I won't go into all that here, but you might find it interesting.

So I had my mid-life awakening, and had rediscovered my creative side, which for some reason I allowed to lapse over the years. I studied Reiki, Tarot, wrote poetry and prose, and photographed the beauty of this sultry coastal Mexican Riviera.

It was a chaotic, transformative time in my life.

Over the next few years, I suffered from continuous sinus infections.

Actually, they started in Whistler in the 90's; I have no idea why. I started taking a common prescription medication, and began to wonder if I was allergic to it. I'd be walking around just fine then I'd suddenly experience shortness of breath.

Finally, after much googling, I correlated the difficulty breathing I was having to the product prescribed to me when I had sinusitis. So I stopped taking it. And the doctor prescribed a different drug.

One morning around five, I woke up and was unable to breathe. I went on like that for maybe a half hour or so. I waited this long because it had happened before and soon, everything would be fine. However, this time, it didn't get better. I got myself dressed, then got in my car and drove myself to a hospital half an hour away.

I called my GP (general practitioner) on the way and told him I must be having an allergic reaction to the newly prescribed sinus drug. I had a similar reaction before with the other drug, and I was sure I simply needed a shot of adrenaline, so I asked if he could have the emergency room doctor ready to administer the shot. He agreed without asking me any questions.

I arrived at the emergency department and was administered the shot. Afterwards I laid down for a while, then got dressed, went to Starbucks, and drove home.

No one did an EKG or took any X-rays. I'm lucky to be alive from this instance alone.

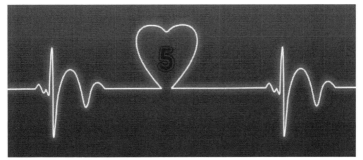

CALIFORNIA DREAMIN'

It was 2007, five years after my big life changes, and Mexico was not the same for me anymore. My mother had died. She was the one who'd believed in me and supported me unconditionally. Whenever I felt down, or second-guessed my decisions, I could call her and she would build me up.

I was no longer in a relationship either. I had craved something — or some*one* — but was unsure exactly what it was I was truly wanting. I loved Mexico, don't get me wrong, but I just *knew* something was missing within my life.

I tried internet dating, which is another book I need to write for sure! I also continued my writing and visited my older son who was graduating from University in Montreal. My two boys have always supported me in all my life decisions, so I was very excited when my younger son joined me in Puerto Vallarta for a while. Then he moved to Cancun, before eventually returning to Canada to become a chef.

By early 2007, I felt it was time for another shift in my life.

I thought about working for a local developer in Puerto Vallarta, but I also had an appointment for an interview with an international company for a sales position, which would have me traveling between Miami and all of Latin America.

But then I thought, *maybe it was time to return to Whistler for a season*. I *visualized* in my mind what doing so might entail.

At this point in my life, I knew what worked for me, and what didn't — both personally and professionally. I had a mental checklist of the things I wanted and went about stating the *intention* in my mind.

Now, let me be clear about this. I made the *final* decision to move on with my life over the period of a week, but I made a checklist of everything I wanted, concerning my change of career, in a parking lot while sitting in my car, just before heading inside for the interview for an international sales position.

Fifteen minutes later, in the middle of this interview, my phone rang. I was completely surprised by the person calling me from Whistler, though I politely suggested my caller should call me back in half an hour.

I loved the idea of the international sales job with the Miami company, but wasn't completely sure I would be comfortable spending so much time on the road. So I politely declined the offer. When I received the call back from Whistler, I was offered the position that checked off every single box on my "must-have" list. Just as I had envisioned.

It was November 2007, and as soon as I accepted the position, I set the same intention in my mind to bring a man into my life. I began searching an online dating service in the Seattle area for a guy that might check off all the boxes on my checklist for the kind of relationship I wanted.

And he appeared.

There was only one thing that would stand in our way, although we didn't know it at the time, and wouldn't until a few months later.

I packed up everything that was important to me, filled the back of my new red Jeep Liberty, and set off on the road trip of my dreams.

Was I crazy to drive all by myself through Mexico and up the Pacific Coast of North America? Yes, probably. But I've always been fearless and impulsive, and maybe on occasion you should be too!

It was the middle of November and I had no set schedule — just a destination and two weeks to get there. The longest road trip I'd ever taken by myself, before this trip, was four hours, so I was pushing my own personal limits. As Tony Robbins would say, "I was taking massive action, determined to take back control of my life."

As it turned out, I would find answers for challenges I didn't yet know existed.

I drove through the states of Nayarit and Sonora in a trance. I always believed the pull of Mexico, for me, was mystical and had to do with the many lives of my soul. All of my own personal beliefs will turn out to be significant, which you will soon see as my story unfolds.

My road trip continued. It took three days to get to the US, and I admit I was a bit nervous and second-guessing myself. I waited in a three-hour sunset lineup at the Nogales border, between Mexico and the United States. My camera captured the wild and rugged Sonoran desert sunset colors and took my breath away.

Eventually, I made it across the border.

I love the dramatic coast of California and had stopped for a day in Manhattan Beach to write a bit of poetry, and nearly froze my butt off in a motel in Marin County.

The Redwood Forest was magical, but I drove through at night and it was eerie. I cherish my photos from the stormy coast of Oregon. I spent time in awe of the bent and weathered grey trees, and the hundreds of seals along the beach.

So many places, so little time. There's a whole world out there that needs to be explored, and even as I write this, I feel like it might be time for another road trip!

Finally, on a rainy black night near the end of November, I was drawing closer to Seattle, ready for my blind date with the internet match. We'd agreed to meet at the Olympic Sculpture Park, but I'd never been to Seattle, and had no idea where the park was.

By early evening, it was completely dark. It was raining, as it so often does in that area, and I was in Federal Way, which is halfway between Tacoma and Seattle.

But my cell phone wouldn't work in the US! *I admit it, I can be a complete ditz!* What was I thinking? There was no way I could find the place I was supposed to meet my internet man, and I never thought to stop and ask anyone.

What a great first and last impression; I stood him up!

I simply gave up and found a motel for the night, and the next day, I arrived in Whistler.

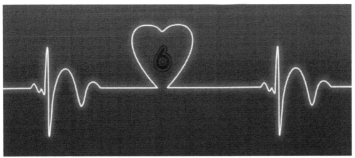

IT'S THE ALTITUDE

"Sacha, I need to stop for a second." Sacha, my youngest son, is a snowboarder and was in far better shape than I!

"What's up, Mom?"

"I think I'm tired from the long drive. I'm out of breath. It's the altitude." I'd been in Whistler for a couple of weeks by this time, but those excuses still seemed quite logical to me (hindsight sarcasm at its best).

My son stood silently above, waiting for me to reach the top of the stairs near the pizza place inside the village.

"I've been living at the beach at sea level. I've got to adjust to Whistler's higher altitude; the mountains, you know?"

Sacha nodded in understanding.

Ten minutes later, I finally made it to the top, and we were soon eating pizza and catching up on each other's lives. Sacha was working as a chef in a trendy restaurant in town and was excited to have his mom around for the winter.

"How's work, Mom?"

"It's not Mexico! Things are more corporate, but I love it. I needed a challenge and a change in my life."

"Do you love your chalet in Emerald? It's not in the village, but I suppose it's okay because you have your car."

"The company came through on all its promises, so yes, I love it. And I can't believe I'm saying I missed the snow!" We both laughed.

"So, you want to try snowboarding with me?"

"Hah, that's not going to happen! I'll photograph *you* though."

My red-headed son smiled and I saw a flash of the child he'd once been. Now however, he was a grown-up man with responsibilities and choices of his own. I wanted to brush the hair from his eyes and wipe away the frown from between his brows. But I knew he'd swat my hand away. So instead, we ate our pizza and made plans to get together another night when he didn't have to work.

After our visit, I drove cautiously toward the northern part of town, strategically avoiding the dangerous black ice. I was in love with the beauty of the workers' lights twinkling along the ski runs as the hills were groomed for the next day. The moon shone a path toward the frozen-over Green Lake, and I couldn't resist pulling over at the lookout to admire the beauty and peace of the night.

I still think of that night and the peace I felt, completely unaware that, over the next thirty days, three separate events were about to change my life forever.

EVENT ONE: MY COWBOY

I'll always remember his faded tan cowboy boots — scuffed, old, comfy — and the sky blue denim shirt stretched taut across powerful broad shoulders — my cowboy, as I refer to him. And I'll definitely never forget that lustful smile on his lips when I answered his knock on my hotel room door.

I was naked... sort of.

I'm not usually that kind of girl... except the times when I am. And that was one of those times. I stood just inside the door to a room with a luxurious king-sized bed, surrounded by floor-to-ceiling glass, on the twenty-eighth floor of the Sheraton Wall Center, and was wrapped in a gauzy pink beach wrap. A girl has to meet a dare, right?

"So even though you're cheating with that pink sheer wrap, I'm impressed." Standing six feet and a few inches, Dr. Evil flashed that silly, young, boyish smile and kissed me softly on my lips.

I brushed stray strands of the softest, dusty-brown hair out of his sexy, grey eyes and laughed, proud of my sophisticated nakedness and ready for wherever the evening would take us.

It may be difficult for you to align your thoughts that a spiritual woman and a "meet me at the door naked" first-date type of girl can exist within one person. But that's who I am. By now, you may have deduced that there is nothing traditional about me.

I don't believe in picket fences, and for some reason, have always been allergic to wedding bands. It's not that I don't *want* to be married. Not at all. I love the idea. I just can't seem to figure out how to make the happily-ever-after part of it work.

But then, as I write these words, one of the secrets of my healing stares right back at me — *How could you love another, Lynda, when you've never really felt you, yourself, was worthy of love?*

Definitely a bad affirmation, but at that time in my life, I still had a lot of self-love issues that needed my attention.

It was December 21, 2007, just four days before Christmas, and in front of me stood my dream man. I had visualized him in my mind, and had written down my wish list of attributes — age appropriate, successful nerd (he even *looks* like Bill Gates), living in Seattle (only because that's the home of Starbucks & Amazon), handsome, fun, and single.

His seventeen-year old daughter and her girlfriends were the ones who'd prepared his online profile — without a photo — on the dating site where I'd stumbled across him. Yes, he'd known about it, sanctioned it even, but they'd had to do the work. They'd tirelessly sifted through numerous responding women, and I was one of their top choices.

After many hours getting to know each other on Skype and Yahoo, as much as two people *can* know each other who've never actually met, there he and I finally were, meeting in person.

As I previously mentioned, our online-relationship began while I was still living in Mexico and I was supposed to stop in Seattle so we could finally meet in person. But I'd gotten lost and stood him up. However, I was forgiven and have been ridiculously infatuated ever since I looked into his mischievous, gentle, grey eyes.

There was also sadness within those eyes. Throughout our

first evening, I learned about the woman he'd loved, who had died a few years before from Multiple Sclerosis. With all my man's scientific brilliance, he cursed himself because he hadn't been able to find the answers to save her.

As our night unfolded, and well into the next day, we shared our pain and our hopes, and continued to build a strong bond. I knew from the first time we chatted online we had something special. And now that we were physically together, I only wanted to hold him and take away his pain.

This would turn out to be a major event in my life. Our time together was magical.

But life has a way…

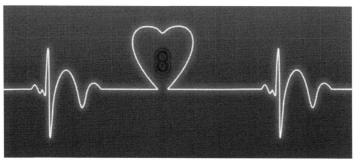

SAIL BOATS AND SANTA CLAUS

"Merry Christmas!" I smiled on Skype. "Where are you?"

"We're on the boat." My cowboy was dressed in casual khaki pants, a plaid shirt, and barefoot.

"What! Aren't you freezing your butt off?"

"Nah, the water's more or less the same temperature in Puget Sound year-round."

"So what are you doing out there?"

"I'm with my daughter. She's crabbing, and I just finished making a pie and putting it in the oven. Christmas dinner."

This was too much. He cooks, he sails, he's super-bright, successful and a great lover! What's the catch?

"And you, Lynda? What are you up to?"

"The usual... writing poetry, hanging out at the chalet with friends, and chatting with you!"

"I'll probably go diving later and do some underwater night photography. I'll show you the shots."

"Are you serious?"

"Of course. Do you dive?"

"No. I barely swim, and I hate the cold. Well, *despise* would be a better word."

When we met in Vancouver, we'd covered a lot of territory. I now knew my man was born on a ranch in New Mexico, and I knew about the sailing, but not the diving, cooking and underwater night photography! I wondered if I'd ever be able to keep up with him.

My cowboy laughed and sipped on a glass of red wine. "I made some decisions since we met."

Oh no, here it comes. We hardly got started, and he's blowing me off already! "Yes?"

"I've resigned from some of the things I've been doing to keep my mind busy. After my wife died, I've tried to keep my mind focused. So between my work and other things, I had no time to feel sorry for myself."

I waited, unsure of where this was going. Afraid. I'd finally met Mr. Right…at least, someone I felt I really wanted to spend time with, but he did come with baggage and issues. Possibly things which might never be resolved.

"But after meeting you, I decided to let some other things go so I'd have more time to get to know you." He grinned — kind of goofy and cocky at the same time — as he waited to see what I'd say.

I wasn't going to say I was planning the wedding yet, but, you know. I've always wanted to wear a Vera Wang wedding gown. The color white might be inappropriate at my age, but she makes colored wedding gowns too, I already checked! But I kept my thoughts to myself.

"That's great! So when will I see you again?"

We talked of other things for a long time, and I could hear noise in the background, and laughter and teasing from his daughter. I bet she was proud of her matchmaking skills.

Eventually, we said our goodbyes, but before we signed off, we planned a date the week after New Years.

I sighed, closed up my computer, and went to join my friends. All was well in my world... until — all of a sudden — it wasn't.

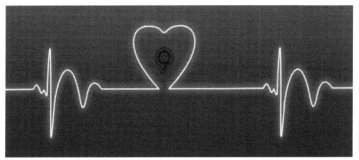

EVENT TWO: EVERY BREATH I TAKE

I paid no attention to the messages my own body was desperately trying to send me until it was almost too late.

I should start at the beginning, but that would assume I knew the exact moment in time when my heart gave up on me.

It was a late Saturday afternoon, soon after Christmas, and I remember how the snow was falling in big, fluffy flakes. I was struggling for breath, making my way up the stairs from the underground cineplex in Whistler.

While I have no recollection of the name of the movie I saw that day, I can still clearly see all the skiers walking around, laughing and bragging about their stunts and accomplishments achieved. People surrounded me, yet not one of them saw I was in distress.

I tried to walk along slowly, beside the shops. I soon had to admit my breathing was not getting any better. Finding a ledge outside The Body Shop — how apropos is that! — I sat for several minutes.

Eventually, my breathing returned to normal, but for the first time since I started having these attacks, it became clear to me that something was wrong with my heart. Still, I walked to the parking lot a couple of blocks away, got into my Jeep and drove myself over to the Town Centre Medical Clinic.

My regular doctor wasn't working that weekend, but Dr. K. knew what was wrong right away. She said nothing of what that was to me though. Instead, she sent me to the Emergency Medical Centre for X-rays.

An hour later, she received the results and revealed what the tests had shown her. "You're in congestive heart failure. You have Dilated Cardiomyopathy."

"Is that serious?"

"Very," she answered with a grave tone. "The radiologist called over to ensure I understood what we were seeing in the X-rays. Your heart is enlarged. I want to start you on a pill to reduce the fluids around your heart and organize an appointment with a cardiologist as soon as possible. We will call Monday with a date for an echocardiogram in Vancouver at Lions Gate Hospital."

"Tell me, Dr. K., what does this *really* mean?"

"Well, a specialist will check the echo of your heart. Then the cardiologist will put you on medications and try to find out why you have this condition. You will both work on healing your heart. Do you smoke?"

"No."

"Drink?"

"Very little."

"Do you have any history of heart problems?"

"Maybe."

"Maybe?"

"Well, maybe about ten years ago... I have to think about that. There must be some records somewhere."

"Well I assume it was fixed, or else it led to this incident."

We both sat silently. From the look on her face, I knew I was in trouble. She watched me with sadness in her eyes. Tears slid slowly down my cheeks.

"I'm so sorry."

I could feel she cared. "Can it be healed?"

She looked away. "It depends on many factors. Your cardiologist will work with you."

"Should I go to the hospital in the city right now?"

"If you start feeling bad again, yes, call an ambulance. But I think with this medication, we should be able to control the symptoms until you can see a cardiologist for additional treatment options."

"Why do I have this? I don't really drink, never smoked or did drugs, never been overweight… I did everything right."

She passed me a tissue to wipe my tears. "I don't know, Lynda. We will just have to do some tests, wait and see."

I sat in my car, alone and afraid. Skiers passed by me, laughing and smiling after a full day of adventure on Whistler Mountain.

How can they laugh when my world is falling apart? Heart Disease. How can this be happening to me?

All I could think about was my sons, my man, and a future that might no longer exist.

I picked up my medication from the pharmacy and drove home alone.

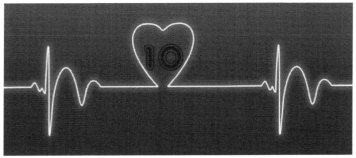

ECHOES

After ten minutes of driving, I was in the north part of the village on Highway 99 when I pulled off at a scenic point to collect my thoughts. Daylight had fallen and the moon was casting a silver glow across frozen Green Lake. Wisps of snow settled gently on the bench around me.

I watched smoke rise from ski chalets dotting Blackcomb Mountain. Grooming machines trailed a ribbon of lights down the slopes as another magnificent ski day was put to rest. At Fitzsimmons Pub, skiers and snowboarders would be telling stories of inhuman physical feats, while consuming pitchers of beer and mounds of nachos with cheese. And all I could think about was death.

But I was too young to die. And besides, whatever was wrong with me had been wrong for a long time, so I must be okay, or I would be dead by now. *Right?*

I thought back to all the other times when I was in the shower trying to catch my breath. Even walking across the sand at Los Muertos Beach in Puerto Vallarta, I'd been gasping for air. And what about the adrenaline shot at the hospital? Really? And the two weeks on the road from Mexico to Canada! What was I thinking? I must be certifiable; I was lucky to be alive.

I pulled into the chalet in Emerald fifteen minutes later. My two girlfriends were in party-mode, preparing for a crazy night at the clubs. Nikki worked at the sex shop in town and was dancing around the room in one of her many costumes. That night, she was a nurse — although I've never seen a nurse with a red plastic miniskirt which barely covered her assets before. Nikki strutted towards me in thigh-high, black-patent leather boots and waved a whip, with a lustful look that had me laughing out loud.

"We're going out tonight and you need to join us! There's a party at the shop and you *must* dress up!"

"Hah, I don't think so!" The girls knew it was almost impossible to get me out to the clubs. I had my heart set on Mr. Right and I wasn't interested in meeting anyone else.

"What have you heard from the doctor?"

I froze and stared at them. *How could they know? I only found out myself an hour ago.* But then I realized they were talking about my man, my PhD doctor, my cowboy. *Not* Dr. K.

"Ah, not much. He's going away on a business trip towards the end of the month. I hope he's back for Valentines Day. We're meeting this weekend in Seattle..." I hesitated, unsure if I could make a trip with my newly-diagnosed condition. "You girls look like you're going to have a wild night. I pity the poor guy that runs into you, Nikki! He's in for an insane time!"

The girls carried on as I grabbed something from the fridge and went to my room. I thought about googling cardiomyopathy. I lit incense instead, pulled out my yoga mat and did a couple of very bad poses, trying to find a quiet and sacred spot within my broken heart, and meditated on life.

Hours later, I turned to God. We've had sort of a love-hate relationship since I'd entered the convent to become a missionary sister at the age of eighteen. It wasn't about my disappointment with monastic life, or the toothbrush I was forced to use to clean the grout on the stairs. It was more about the Church not approving of my life choices; I was definitely not prepared to "work on" a marriage, which had lasted a mere six months, culminating with a frustrated husband who'd tried to smother me with a pillow. Divorced and excommunicated from the Catholic religion because of said divorce, at the age of twenty-one, just plain sucked. So you might say I'm not a fan of *organized* religion.

God and I had a conversation of sorts. I cursed. I said I've got far too many things I want to do with my life and a love I want to explore. I tried bargaining, begging for time…and then I let it all go and went to sleep.

The following weekend, I drove to Seattle and my cowboy took me on a date to St. Michel Winery. I didn't drink red wine but was willing to try it to please him. He told me he had a thousand-bottle wine cellar and a library of author-signed first edition books. I realized he was eccentric in too many ways to list. Yet the more we shared, the more I knew I'd found a man with whom I wanted to build a life.

We took photos that are forever embedded in my heart — especially the scuffed cowboy boots. We talked about his daughter, and I could see how much he loved her. And we made plans of things we wanted to do when he came back from his business trip. I felt love and loved, and for a brief moment in time, I pretended I would have a future.

I never told him about my heart.

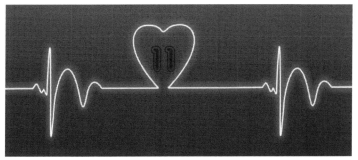

EMERGENCY ROOMS AND OTHER DEPRESSING PLACES

"I'm not getting undressed!"

The nurse looked up in annoyance. "But this is an emergency room. You need to get undressed so the specialist can examine you."

I stood stubbornly facing the admitting nurse. It was eight-thirty in the evening and I'd arrived at Lions Gate Hospital in North Vancouver — a two-hour drive from Whistler — for the echocardiogram at ten that morning. I was tired, hungry, *really* upset and I wanted to go home.

As it turned out, even with a serious heart condition, it was still a two-week wait to see a cardiologist in Vancouver, but the echocardiogram could be performed within ten days of the appointment.

After the echocardiogram, I waited a further half hour. *How long does it take for the technician to verify that the test was done properly?*

Finally, a doctor appeared and informed me that I was in very serious congestive heart failure and must see the specialist as soon as possible. They would call for him. I was then sent to the emergency room, where I would sit and wait while broken bones and other "real emergencies" were looked after.

I sat in my corner and cried silent tears. *This can't be happening to me*. I was in denial.

I almost walked out a couple of times, but what good would that do? Is the medical system broken in Canada? Maybe. Was I an emergency or not? I waited and waited.

After almost ten hours, the broken bones were fixed and the "real emergencies" were taken care of, and the nurse finally called me to a curtained-off section of the emergency room, then proceeded to ask me to undress. I refused. She shook her head and said the doctor would be with me shortly.

A series of interns, doctors, and nurses wandered by my area, all looking to catch a glimpse of the girl in the emergency room who had refused to put on a gown. Finally, Dr. M. showed up.

"Why won't you put on a robe?" he asked with a smile.

I think he already had my number. I mean, you never argue with a redhead, right? I went into my story about how long I waited to see him, how tired and hungry I was, so he quickly pulled up my file and began reading. Then he asked me all the routine questions about smoking, alcohol, and family history. At one point, he frowned.

"Your Ejection Fraction is 28%. Let me explain what that means. This is the way we measure how well the left ventricle of your heart is pumping out blood. A normal heart is 50-70%. You are in serious heart failure. I want to keep you in overnight for observation."

I rolled my eyes, which I'm well-known for doing. "Look, whatever is going on, can you give me meds? I feel fine. I don't want to stay overnight. If I needed to stay overnight, it should have been last week when I couldn't breathe!"

Dr. M. sighed and shook his head. "Okay, we'll do it your way. Here are your prescriptions; fill them as soon as possible.

Keep taking what Dr. K. prescribed. And I will arrange these other tests as soon as possible."

I nodded, afraid to say anything.

"This is very serious, Lynda. We're going to do a nuclear test to check things out. And a few other tests." He smiled kindly once again.

"I'm not the first patient you've seen with this, right?"

"No."

"What's the prognosis?"

Dr. M. hesitated, then looked me in the eyes. "We have to remain positive, make some lifestyle changes, eat well, try walking, as long as it doesn't make you short of breath. Time will tell if you respond to medication."

I brushed away those damn tears again.

"I'll see you next week in my office."

I left the hospital and drove the two and a half hour trip back to Whistler alone.

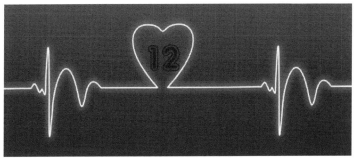

SWOLLEN HEART

The next morning, I had a conversation with myself. I thought about throwing a pity party, but who would I invite? At this point, only one of my coworkers knew my situation. He wasn't a close friend — I don't have *close friends* — but he was someone who needed to know my situation in case anything happened at work. He was kind and had talked me through the wait in the emergency room. He called and texted throughout the day to be sure I was okay, and that was special for me. Without his support, I probably would have walked out.

So who should I tell about my problem? And why?

I did tell some family members. After all, the doctor said it might be hereditary. Instead of bluntly coming out and asking for support, I instead gave them the message *check your heart*.

I got back this response, "I work out everyday and my heart is strong. So thanks for telling me, but I'm good."

And my older bro said, "I fly and take medicals every year. So I'm fine."

And my boys... Let's just say that they have their own lives and their own challenges.

I was pretty much on my own. I've always been a loner, and you reap what you sow.

It's not like I was on my deathbed, so all must be good,

right? Maybe family would have been there for me if I'd let anyone in. I closed myself up tight, and this "mama kept her drama to herself."

And then there's my cowboy. At this point in my life, this man was my dream guy. He was everything I wanted and then some. It's not like I didn't have the experience to know the difference between *throw-away-lovers* and *keepers*. But in those early moments in our relationship he'd told me about the woman he couldn't save, the one who'd died. I could clearly see all that pain and sadness in his eyes. My guy was a single dad with a very intense career — one he talked around, over and under, never really saying the kind of science he worked on.

I let the subject drop and told myself I wouldn't have known what he was talking about anyway. He was private about some things, and so was I, which is why I made the decision not to tell him about my heart.

On a chilly morning not long after the ER trip, on my way to work, I stopped for my coffee at Second Cup in Whistler. The sun was streaming through the windows, and the aroma of roasted beans is one of my favorite things. I smiled at Wendy, the owner, and took my first sip of white chocolate mocha. I think I purred.

I looked out the window and watched the first skiers on Blackcomb Mountain come racing down the fresh morning powder, and my thoughts turned to my guy. I realized I could never tell my cowboy what was going on. He had said during our first evening together he would *never* go through that again; he'd never watch someone he loved die and be helpless to save her.

So I kept it all inside. My heart became swollen even more… only now it contained fear, loneliness, and disappointment.

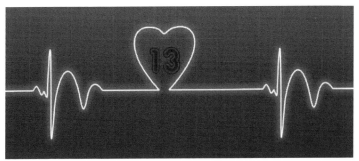

THE RHYTHM IS BROKEN

What do you do with a broken heart?

I was so sick and tired of doctors asking me if I drink or smoke. No I don't. I've never smoked, could never even stand the smell. The hippy-stoner peace-thing was not *my* thing; I was someone who needed to be in control too much to do drugs or just let go. I was busy opening businesses, designing clothes, reading books on how to run a business — my majors in the arts didn't help me with that.

I did everything the doctors said, but I was already doing those things before. I didn't really need to lose weight, but stress? Well, everyone has stress, don't they? How do you handle stress if you don't drink or smoke weed? I'm joking. If you have a life, you've got stress.

I went back to see my regular doctor at the Whistler Medical Centre. "Have you got my test results yet?" *Dr. K was a temporary weekend doctor and my regular GP had returned.*

"Yes. It's what we thought; you do have a severe case of Idiopathic Dilated Cardiomyopathy. Are you taking your meds?"

"Of course."

"How do you feel?"

"I'm good. I've not had an incident since I was diagnosed."

"Well, keep doing what you're doing. Time will tell."

"What does that mean? Is there a cure? Will I get better?" I swiped those damn tears off my cheeks.

The doctor looked at me. He was an Irish gentleman around my age. "Have you anyone to talk to Lynda?"

I remained silent as the tears dribbled down my cheeks and simply shook my head.

"Here." He handed me a card for a therapist in the village. "I hear good things about her. Make an appointment; she will help you deal with how you're feeling."

I said my goodbyes and headed out into the sunlight. I stopped to think and looked at the name on the card. Talking with her didn't *feel* like the right thing for me to do. So I tossed the card into the nearest garbage pail…then went around the corner in search of the Oracle Shop where the psychics do readings!

Kelly, the owner of the store, has the most magnificent, silky, whitest grey hair I've ever seen. Gasp-worthy. Don't laugh.

She was busy chatting with a gentleman about crystals, when she noticed me waiting by the bookshelves and called over, "How can I help you?"

"A friend of mine, Tina, told me to come in here and ask for Krista. She does readings?"

"Yes, of course. She'll be finished with a client in five minutes if you wish to see her?"

"Perfect."

My hands stroked the cover of Louise Hay's classic book *You Can Heal Your Life*.

I remembered buying this book when it first came out. I was at a New Age convention with my sister, back around 1984. I thought of some of the mystical areas and New Age-thinking I've explored in my past. So I picked the book up and looked for the meaning of heart disease —

Lack of joy, dealing with issues from anger, not love.

Affirmation: My heart beats to the rhythm of love

I heard my name and turned.

"You must be Lynda, Tina told me you'd be coming by." A petite blond in her twenties, with a delightful Aussie accent, smiled like she'd known me forever. She immediately took my hand and led me into her private client room.

Now I'm as skeptical as the next person, and I was here about my heart, so I silently went into a mode of healing called Reiki, which I'd studied in the late nineties. I said some of the phrases, imagined the symbols in my mind, and cleared the room of any negative energy.

Krista was organizing a dish of crystals, chattering away, and suddenly stopped. "Did you just Reiki the room?" Krista's eyes glowed with knowing and excitement.

Hah! I'd allowed my intuition to lead me to Krista. I knew then I'd found a sacred place. Which was fortunate, because I had no time. I needed to figure this issue out fast.

I admit I was fearful and desperate. I now believe Krista was a catalyst, a turning point in my struggle. She listened and encouraged me to take control over my heart and my healing.

I NEVER PROMISED YOU A ROSE GARDEN

No you didn't, God. But here I am, a mere mortal trying to deal with living, certain it's not my time to die.

So what did I do, and what do I continue to do?

I wish I could tell you "only one thing" that changed my life and healed me. If I had that answer, we wouldn't need all these mortal beings to work with us, diagnose us, and help us heal.

Why do some people heal and others die? I don't have those answers. And whatever I say is not meant to replace what the doctors are telling you to do, or your belief in a Higher Power who controls your destiny. I'm not a medical doctor. I'm simply a woman who was told in 2008 to get her affairs in order, because she was not responding to medication. But since so many of you have asked, I will try to tell you what I did. It's a combination of what I did and continue to do, but most important it's *how I think.*

I wanted to share my backstory to help you understand how I got to the point where I'm at today. It's been ten years or more, and I have no idea how many years I walked around with the disease undiagnosed.

At this moment in time, my heart pumps normally, except I still have a wonderful little "sigh." My heart skips beats, which is called "arrhythmia" and refers to any change from the normal sequence of electrical impulses. The electrical impulses may happen too fast, too slowly, or erratically – causing the heart to beat too fast, too slowly, or erratically.

But it doesn't hurt. I only feel it when I'm sitting in silence, reading, or lying in bed. It's my *sigh.* For me, it's magical. It reminds me to stop, take a moment to thank my Higher Power for being alive, to be in love with life, and finally, to be able to write this story for you.

Let me continue. I hope you will find some comfort, understanding and guidance through the actions I took, and continue to take each day, for your own healing journey.

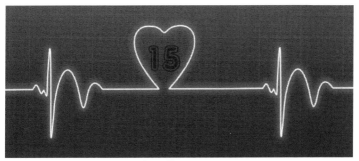

IN DENIAL

Krista, my psychic spiritual healer, helped me center myself. I felt calm and ready to move forward after speaking with her. She was so kind. And in her kindness and laughter, I felt comfort. I don't remember what we did exactly, but I do remember the following conversation.

"You have a powerful ally over your right shoulder — Archangel Raphael. He's the healer — and his wingspan over you, protecting you, is incredibly large. I have never seen him like this before."

I sat in peace for the first time since I'd been diagnosed with congestive heart failure. I had power in my house. We spent a long time talking.

"I've given you some techniques for visualization, and I want you to write in a journal. And when you're ready, come back to see me."

I hugged her like I've known her my whole life. I'd been guided to her and felt I could see clearly now. I was certain I had found the right place; it was time for me to do the work.

INTERNATIONAL AUTHORITIES

When I finally allowed myself to start online research, I was devastated. The news was grim and grimmer. In 2008, one major heart authority after another said cardiomyopathy cannot be healed. The best outcome one can expect is a five-year lifespan. If you are healthy enough, you might have a heart transplant, but there's no guarantee on the results, and the waiting list is long. There are also defibrillators that can be inserted which can help... and on and on.

No wonder my intuition told me *not* to research the subject!

That was in 2008. Now, in 2017, I did some online research again. The sites are more ambiguous this time around. A world-famous hospital still maintains the disease can't be healed. It makes me so sad to read this!

How can a doctor be God? How can a responsible physician or group of specialists make such an inaccurate blanket statement? It leaves people feeling helpless, hopeless, and totally destroyed.

Maybe that's why so many have found my YouTube videos and email me for advice. At least they know there's one person out there that beat a six-month "get your affairs in order" prognosis and is around to tell the story.

So here we go...

Guideline Number One:

Don't believe everything you read online. Be in denial of all the doomsayers.

YOU ARE NOT YOUR DIAGNOSIS

We all have our own stories. We get to pick and choose trials and tribulations from our past to hang our present on. We call that our "biography" and we use it for all kinds of things.

A friend said to me the other day, "I get that from my dad; it's in my genes."

What a pathetic excuse for bad habits or things that can destroy your life! You know what I'm talking about. You hear it everyday in so many ways. "My parents did this... therefore, I am like..." and "My ex did that... therefore, my kids are like this..."

I'm sure there are scientists who will argue the fine points of medicine on this subject. I don't care. Get used to me saying that and repeat after me... *I don't care.*

Everything we say and do in our lifetime is a "choice." We get to design our lives.

If you need proof, look around you. Take any world leader, any guru, any powerful person, and listen to how their lives started, and who they have become — Oprah, Tony Robbins, Dr. Wayne Dyer, the list is endless. They tell their story to show you that your past does not have to define your present.

In the case of *dis-ease*, you get to choose how you react to it. If you buy into the terms of your diagnosis and give away your *power* to make a correction within your body, then you're leaving out a vital part in your healing process.

Don't keep talking about how sick you are, you're only re-enforcing your illness. Stop it! People don't want to hear it. Everyone has his and her own life to live.

I know this is harsh; I've been there. We all want sympathy, but everyone's seen far worse on reality TV. They're not shocked, my friend. Nothing shocks a desensitized world. *Nothing.* So stop looking for sympathy; stop telling your story.

Listen to your doctors, take the appropriate steps, do the work, then make a commitment to yourself to *not* buy into your history or your current story.

Do not *become* your diagnosis. Do not be defined by your disease.

Guideline Number Two:

Make up a new story, one of vibrancy and healing.

"AND THAT HAS MADE ALL THE DIFFERENCE."

I shall be telling this with a sigh
Somewhere ages and ages hence:
Two roads diverged in a wood, and I—
I took the one less traveled by,
And that has made all the difference. —**Robert Frost**

Life is full of choices. Everyday we have option number one, or option number two. Most things we do by rote like driving a car, or walking down the aisles of the grocery store.

When it comes to our bodies, we know right and wrong, but that doesn't necessarily mean we make the right choices. Doctors speak their own special language. We don't always want to take their advice. Then, sometimes, they hit on the right words that resonate within you. I had a doctor like that and his words *made all the difference*.

After several months of treatment, and no response whatsoever to any of the medications, I was in a sad and fearful place.

"In layman's words," my cardiologist said, "you have a swollen heart. The pump is not working at full capacity. The valves aren't opening and closing the way they're supposed to. That's why you have an ejection fracture of 28%."

Leaving Vancouver and driving up to Whistler, it hit me. I

have a *swollen* heart. Of course I do. I will take full responsibility for that.

Why was that conversation so significant? In my case, I believed I've always lived a "heart-centered" life. Then again, maybe I haven't.

Have I confused you yet? This is where epiphanies happen. I started to make a series of statements to myself. Maybe it was out loud, after all, it's a two and a half hour drive to get back to Whistler and I was alone in my car.

My earliest memories are blank, or as I used to say "blocked." I know that's a terrible affirmation and it has been stricken from my vocabulary as part of my healing process. I never felt the need to go back to those years. Whatever happened is history.

Imagine though, all the "heart issues" building up inside of my *physical heart* to the point where my heart was so *swollen* it could not keep pumping blood in a normal manner. What if that swollen heart was unshed tears — unforgiven hurts, past relationship disappointments. What if…?

Now my diagnosis started to make perfect sense to me. The doctor still couldn't find a physical reason, that's why it's called "idiopathic," meaning, *We don't know why you have it, you just do.*

Now I had something to work with.

As I stated, today I refuse to dwell on past hurts. That's against my personal belief. Your biography becomes your biology. So I set about sending light, love, and forgiveness. I burnt incense and found sacred places in nature to breathe in love and let go of hurt. I wrote it out in poetry and prose. And I let it all go.

I know many of you may have skepticism and resistance to

this theory, and I understand that. Be skeptical or be open; it's a choice. If you have read this far, I'm going to presume you're either open or desperate.

A few years earlier, I started writing poetry again, something I hadn't done since I was in my twenties. I wrote more poetry on my solo-driving trip from Mexico to British Columbia months before I was diagnosed. Writing and journaling were easy for me. I could write, *screaming out my frustration and pain* in word bites.

I also like to burn things. I would take a metal bowl or pot, add some dried sage, stash page after page of hurt or pain, send out love and forgiveness, and burn it.

I even took old boyfriends' photos — *any* memories I was holding onto which hurt me and no longer served my heart — and I burned them too.

Release. Breathe.

Let it all go.

Get rid of the weight, pain, and hurts holding you back.

Guideline Number Three:

Write it out, then burn it!

EVENT THREE: BROKEN PICKET FENCES

My cowboy disappeared.

After our first weekend in Seattle, I was hooked — well, you can probably tell I was infatuated with my guy somewhere between Skyping and Meet Me Naked — so I was really looking forward to our date after he came back from his business trip.

That date never happened.

A week-long business trip became four months. My friend, my cowboy, was injured and spent months recovering in a foreign hospital. When he returned to the US, he spent more time living in hospitals than in his own home. He was in no position to continue many things in his life. I, unfortunately, was one of those things.

Did I tell you he's a Taurus? He's a whole new level of stubborn. He would fight his diagnosis, but he would do it alone — his decision, his choice.

When you visualize things in your life, you need to be *very* specific. I forgot to ask the universe to send me a man who was healthy and available, body and soul. They say when man plans, God laughs. This must have been one of those cosmic jokes, but I wasn't in the mood for anymore of them in my life.

I added that pain to my disappointments and wrote it all out, and would continue to write about it for a few years after. I did see him one or two times more. I drove up to Seattle and stayed at one of my favorite hotels. If he was well enough to see me, he did. But I could tell he was trying so hard to hide how much he was suffering.

I remember the day he told me there was no cure for what was wrong with him. He could not, or would not, tell me what was going on. I could see the weariness and pain when he turned away. He was searching for answers and his health became his only focus. Life can take many twists and turns. Mine sure did. In the meantime, because my friend was in a major battle to save his life, I never told him about my heart.

I never told him that my cardiologist called me into his office and told me he was considering surgery. I didn't want to add to the burdens my cowboy already carried. I was in love with this man and desperately wanted him to heal. I couldn't see I was, once again, bottling up something extremely important to me, for the good of someone else.

♥♥♥♥♥

"What! Surgery? What kind of surgery? I don't want any operations."

"Look, your heart is not responding to medication. Your radium test and your echocardiogram show zero improvement. I want to put this defibrillator under your skin near your heart." The doctor showed me this flat metal object about two inches in diameter.

"Wait a minute. Where will that go?"

"Right here. It will sit right under your skin and show a little bump, right above your heart."

"No. No. Absolutely not." I shook my head. "You don't understand. I'm returning to Mexico and I wear bikinis! It's not sexy."

My doctor smiled, though it was more of a sad smile. "Look, Lynda, I don't know what else to do." He looked at me, hesitated, then continued, "Your diagnosis is not good. You need to get your affairs in order."

I sat there stunned as he wrote an appointment with the surgeon on a slip of paper. In his mind, the decision was made.

"He will schedule your surgery, but will meet with you first in three weeks time."

I walked out of his office in Vancouver feeling alone and frightened. I kept saying to myself, it's not my time to die. But all of a sudden, I was afraid that maybe it was.

I drove back to Whistler feeling sorry for myself and decided to stop at the Whistler Medical Centre to talk with Dr. T. He was my local doctor and not a heart specialist, but my instinct told me to talk with him. That conversation would change the direction of my life.

Guideline Number Four:

Let your intuition guide you. Your head and your heart can sometimes be unreliable. Your intuition, your gut, is seldom wrong.

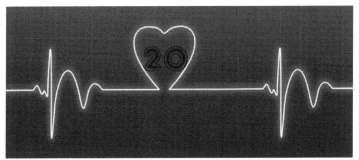

THE WISDOM OF MY ANCESTORS

"I had a patient many years ago, a woman around your age." Dr. T. looked over his spectacles, while I sat uncomfortably on a diagnostic table. His normally smiling Irish eyes stared intensely. He held the results of my latest heart tests in his slight, aging hands. "She was diagnosed incurable by her doctors."

He took his glasses off and wiped them, then looked up at me, as if he were about to impose a death sentence. "Do you know what she told me?"

I shook my head, trying to control my emotions and my damn tears.

"She said, 'I'm not going to die!' and left my office."

I took a deep sigh and finally asked, "What happened?"

"She'd had enough of the doctors and their prognosis, and took her healing into her own hands."

I leaned forward, eager, yet terrified, to learn what happened to the woman.

"She's still alive today." He looked up slyly, with that impish grin I've come to love, and wished me well on my journey.

I will never forget that moment, nor many others that were to follow.

Guideline Number Five: You're not dead yet! Don't accept a death sentence while you're still alive.

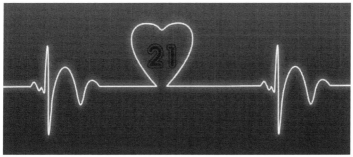

EMPATH(Y)

"You should go to Sedona." Tessa, a vivacious sweet friend, finally got me to talk about what was happening in my life.

She's an Empath — she can *feel* other's pain or energy. She sensed my fear and knew I was troubled, *heart troubled.* As I've said, I told people more on a need-to-know basis. I didn't want anyone's false sympathy. No one could take this journey except me. I also did not want to "become my diagnosis."

I can't tell you how many times I said to myself, "I am *not* my diagnosis." I didn't want that label in my heart or in my head. I've watched too many people *become* their illness.

You know what I'm talking about. Think of the people in your life who have illnesses or dis-ease. They often use those things as an excuse for not going places, not living their lives, and just waiting around for certain death.

Why would someone choose to live that way? That's not *living.* It's *dying* before you're dead!

Yes, I feel very strongly about this. I've been in sales and dealt with all kinds of people over the last forty years. I have to tell you, sometimes I want to shake them and yell at them to *live their lives*!

Tessa and I sat in silence. I felt her presence and her healing energy wash over my emotions.

"Lynda, you should go to Sedona. Work with a healer."

"I've never been to Sedona. I don't even know how to get there. I know I shouldn't travel too. The doctors will freak out."

I could see she wanted to say something, but she kept silent.

After a few moments of silence, I gave in. "Okay. Let me book a trip. I'm going as soon as possible. Will you come with me?"

"This is a journey you need to take on your own."

Five days later, I boarded a flight out of Vancouver International Airport for Phoenix, Arizona. I was on a quest to find my soul — even though I didn't know it at the time.

Guideline Number Six:

Listen to your soul and your intuition. You don't have to do the heavy lifting all by yourself.

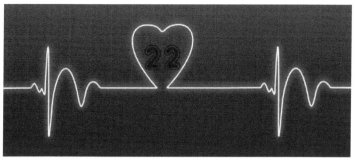

DOUBLE TROUBLE

I scheduled time to stop at a small resort situated on a golf course in Mesa, Arizona, where I had planned to spend four days just relaxing beside a pool. It was November, so it was cold and rainy in Whistler, and Sedona was going to be chilly, but Mesa was filled with sunshine.

I arrived late in the afternoon and found a lounger by the pool. The area was quiet, except for at least fifty black birds sitting on a wire between two poles about fifty yards away. I sighed and watched them for a few minutes. Then I closed my eyes, kept them closed for a couple of minutes, and opened them again.

There was no mistake, I was seeing double. Two lines, two sets of birds. I sat in utter silence, trying to remain calm and refusing to acknowledge what I was seeing. I was tired, but surely it was only the pressure of a full-time career, the flying, and a very tired heart. That's what I was here for right?

I waited several minutes, but still my vision was doubled.

A half hour later, nothing had changed. I returned to my room and changed clothes. I googled hospitals and drove myself to the nearest one. Upon hearing my history, I was moved immediately into a testing area, and from there, to a stroke ward. I was kept overnight for observation.

On day two, the cardiologist came into my room and told me

how weak my heart was. He told me they could see no reason for the double vision — which now was back to normal — but it was a possibility I'd had a mini stroke.

"You shouldn't be traveling. Go home! Don't you realize how serious your heart condition is?"

After countless tests, therapy, and hours spent listening to unhappy middle-aged nurses who were stressed-out by their careers, I was released from the hospital with a new pill to add to my medications. The doctor did not change my prescriptions, nor did he find anything new that I didn't already know about. He also didn't offer me any hope, just a lecture on how irresponsible I was being.

I bought the pill — I called it a horse pill because it was *huge* — and really didn't want to take it. My intuition said no, my doctor said yes. I took it before bed and the next morning, I woke up with the room spinning, and I was vomiting and shaking. This time I called the front desk, they called the paramedics, and I was soon back in the same hospital, but in intensive care this time.

After twenty-four hours, my symptoms went away and I was moved back to — you got it! — the stroke ward. Same doctor, same nurses, same therapy. Stomach virus? Allergic to the pill? Still no answers. This time the doctor was super-nasty, justifiably so, when he found out I was still planning on going to Sedona.

After two days, I was released. Those four days beside the pool had turned into four days in the hospital. My travel plans were looking like a Stephen King movie. But I'm stubborn. I got in my car and started my drive to Sedona. I was weak, frightened and worried that my heart might explode as the altitude rose to almost forty-four hundred feet.

I was committed to healing, and I wouldn't stop until I'd exhausted everything my intuition told me to do — even if I died trying.

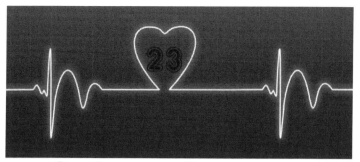

RED ROCKS AND THUNDERSTORMS

I drove into town at sundown, feeling weak after twenty-four hours of vomiting. I was frightened, but I knew I was *supposed* to be there. My drive was otherworldly, filled with light and dark and spirits helping me make this journey. I kept repeating to myself I would be okay.

One highway in, then turn right after a few blocks. "You will see the sign, even in the dark."

And I did.

The first documented human presence in Sedona, Arizona dates back to between 11,500 and 9000 BC. The first uncovering of native artifacts related to their presence was in 1995. Can you imagine the energy of thousands of years of bloodshed and healing that have taken place on these lands? I could *feel* the soul of Sedona from the moment I neared the town.

Sedona is surrounded by the most incredible red rock formations. It's a place of transition, of finding oneself or losing oneself. For me, it was a place for the not-quite-whole, the lonely, and the confused. Sedona is known to hold some of the world's most powerful energy vortexes.

I came because I was desperate, and my intuition told me this place might help me save my life.

I awoke the next morning tired, feeling lethargic, but ready. I looked out my main floor window and saw Oak Creek running slowly through the canyon. Huge red rock formations had chipped off and fallen along the banks. The sky was overcast, and it looked like a storm was brewing.

The condo resort where I was staying provided a light, buffet breakfast. It was also an opportunity to hear about the area and decide what types of adventures I might like to take.

A very young woman had brochures with titles that read *Pink Jeep Tours*, *Hiking Through the Canyons*, *A Visit to the Shops*, and *Cultural Center*.

A small group of twenty or so signed up for the different activities, while I sat sipping coffee and eating a muffin.

Nothing she talked about had appealed to me. I thought about my cozy condo and the fireplace and a good book. I didn't feel well enough to do much more than that.

Everyone else was leaving, and I was just standing there, uncertain what to do next.

The young woman picked up her brochures and packed them away. She looked up at me for a moment, and with a huge smile, said, "What can I do for you?"

"I have no idea."

Sedona is a mystical place. I wanted to go inside myself, not explore the area. I knew I needed to experience Sedona in a totally different way.

After several seconds, she said, "I know! You need to spend time with Akal."

I had no idea what that meant. Nor did I question her judgment. I simply followed my intuition and said, "Okay..."

"I will call him right now and see when he can come over."

An hour later, I was being driven along the streets of Sedona in a dusty, tan-colored Jeep. My driver, Akal — a rugged forty-something man wearing a *Raiders of the Lost Ark* hat — laughed and smiled while he pointed out the main points of interest in town. I told myself everything was going to be okay.

That day, in November of 2008, was when the next event occurred which changed my life forever.

Menacing clouds rolled in over the imposing giant, red rock vortexes, turning everything dark. I wondered where we were going and why. But the words, *Let go and let God,* were running through my thoughts.

The Jeep made the ten-minute trip up to Airport Vortex. A vortex is a location, a place in nature, where the earth energy swirls and draws to its center everything that surrounds it, like a tornado. There are five major vortexes in Sedona, but the Airport Vortex is a favorite.

Akal took a blanket, a giant umbrella, and a drum from the trunk of his Jeep and we began our ascent to a ridge overlooking Bell Rock and the valley. I went slowly — worried I couldn't make the fifteen-minute walk. But I did it.

All this time, Akal talked about his life and his many years of shamanic studies. He'd lived in Sedona for most of that time and often took people out to explore the red rock formations, the caves, the area's history, and the various vortexes.

He never asked me why I'd made the journey to Sedona. We talked about life and spirit and it's place in our lives.

After an hour or so, the dark skies told me it might be time to leave, but Akal merely smiled, pulled out the huge umbrella, and gave it to me to hold. The skies opened up and poured down on the red rock, creating rivulets of red water... the color of a heart.

Instead of leaving like normal people might do in the middle of a storm, Akal asked if it would be okay if he drummed. I think back now and wonder if it was his way of asking me if I was ready to take a risk, ready to allow him to call in those missing pieces. You might not be ready for this discussion. If you resist, that's okay. It's not your time to hear this…yet. But let me also say, the things we resist the most, are likely those things we need to hear and do.

Here's what I have come to understand. Over our lifetimes — and maybe past lives, if you believe in that concept — our souls become fractured. Certainly, in this lifetime, we allow so much anger, pain, and hurt to inhabit our hearts and souls. It builds up.

Over and over again we try to accept, forgive, move on. Yet sometimes, we don't. And it piles on until our hearts are swollen and unable to function. Our breath is literally taken away from us.

The shaman, Akal, called out to retrieve the broken pieces of my soul. He called them back and made my *emotional* heart and soul whole again.

When I arrived in Sedona, I was breathless and broken, and a part of my soul was missing. Every breath I take today, I look back on that day and thank whatever Higher Power was present in that moment. I knew — without knowing how or what he did — that I was healed.

The skies stopped pouring, the clouds formed into a heart above me, and the sun shone through.

When I walked down from that vortex, my step was light. My heart beat normally again... and *I knew it*.

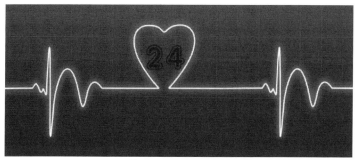

STRONGHEART

Akal had given me the name Strongheart.

I had forgotten that. And today, as I share my story, there are things going on in my life that require a strong heart.

"I promise you, Akal, I will never forget the amazing name you bestowed on me that day. I will live up to it over the future decades of my life."

He told me there were two books he suggested I read. One is called *Matrix Energetics: The Science and Art of Transformation* by Richard Bartlett. The other is *The Three "Only" Things: Dreams, Coincidence & Imagination* by Robert Moss.

I still have challenges reading the "science" of it all. It's definitely more than I need or want to absorb, except in small increments. I've never approached my healing from a scientific-base of "What we know to be true." Instead, I've delved into the ancient ways and what we "intuit" to be true. I leave the science to the physicians, the PhDs, those who work with facts. However, more today than ten years ago, those lines are blurring.

I inscribed the book by Robert Moss Akal had given me that day with *November 4, 2008, Akal and Lynda Strongheart.*

Then I wrote *I ask for the health my body needs/requires to serve the purpose of my Soul.*

I spent the rest of my week visiting the other vortexes. I took long walks, read, and wrote. I visited the New Age Centre and touched the crystals, engaged the psychics, and used healing mantras throughout my waking hours.

And most importantly, I found a home at Picazzo's Organic Italian Kitchen! The bartender made magical Sangria, and the chef concocted spectacular organic pizzas. The work I did on the inside definitely increased my appetite for food and drink.

Life was mellow, and life was good. *I* was the change that needed to happen within my healing.

Finally, I prepared to return to Canada.

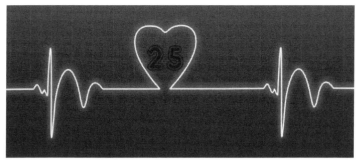

DOCTORS AND DOCTORATES

The plane landed smoothly at Vancouver International Airport. I grabbed my bags and found my car in the long-term parking lot. A sense of peace and wellness filled my heart.

I pulled out my cell phone and called my specialist's office, and he answered out of breath, rushing as usual, overworked by the Canadian Health Care System.

"Hi, Doc!"

"What's up, my friend? Are you okay?"

"I have a favor to ask."

"Of course."

"I know I have an appointment coming up with the surgeon, but before I go, I want to do the MUGA test a second time."

"Why?"

"Because."

I didn't want to get into the Sedona thing with him, or the double vision, or the four days in the hospital in Arizona. That was a face-to-face conversation for a later time.

"Okay, I trust you know why you want it. My nurse will call you to confirm."

I spent a few sleepless nights, but that had become the norm for me. One of the changes in my life was sleep. I would be up twenty-four hours, and still work each day and carry on with my life. It was strange, but everything about my life during that period was unusual.

Within the week, I entered the now familiar room for Nuclear Imagery Testing in Lions Gate Hospital. A receptionist nodded recognition toward me, handed me a form to fill out, and gave me a gown to change into.

This time I was excited to move forward and didn't protest the gown.

A young man explained the procedure from beginning to end to me, and I didn't bother telling him I'd been through his tunnel before, freaked out and frightened.

This time, I simply smiled and nodded, then the procedure began.

A multi-gated acquisition (MUGA) scan creates video images of the lower chambers of the heart that hold blood (called "ventricles") to check whether they are pumping blood properly. It shows any abnormalities in the size of the ventricles and in the movement of the blood through the heart.

The technologist will ask you to lie still on a table and place a special camera above your chest. The camera is about three feet wide and uses gamma rays to track the nuclear tracer. As the tracer moves through your bloodstream, the camera will take pictures to see how well the blood is pumping through your body. The pictures will be taken from many different views, and each one lasts about five minutes.

A nuclear medicine technologist who has been specially trained and certified to conduct the test performs it. A radiologist or a nuclear medicine physician oversees the technologist. And a radiologist interprets the scan results.

By the way, do *not* try to cross the border into the United States after such a test. The nuclear sensors can see the nuclear stuff. Baby, that makes you *hot...* in a *very bad* way! In today's world, with the fear of terrorism, it's particularly important to keep in mind what you do and where you go for a day or two after this test.

Typically, you won't receive any results from this procedure without several people first reviewing the scan. Everything must go through your cardiologist. I knew this, so I spent time flirting and chatting up the technologist and the male radiologist. It paid off.

The technologist came out and told me all the images were clear and it was exactly what they needed.

Then he said the words I will cherish until the day I die.

"But why are you having this test? Your heart seems very healthy with an ejection fracture of 68%. But please don't say anything. It needs to be read by the senior radiologist. I'm just a technician; he might see something I missed. I'll have him check your results right away and send them to your family physician and cardiologist."

He didn't need to know my biography. All he needed was to feel the healing energy that was swirling around me, and the gratitude that lit up my eyes.

I silently thanked my Higher Power, hugged my technologist hard, and left.

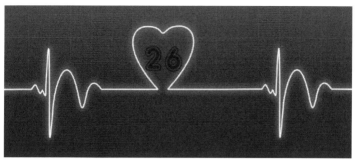

ARCHANGELS AND SPIRITS

I'm Irish. Of *course* I believe in spirits — and not only the ones you drink!

I studied Reiki, an ancient Japanese-form of healing, for several years. I admit to being a dilettante. I'll take a little of this, a prayer or two from there, and mix it all up in my wonderful spiritual cocktail. My numerology tells me I'm highly psychic or intuitive, but this is not news to me. Signs from the universe have always surrounded me.

A week had passed since I'd returned to Whistler from Sedona. The following week I was scheduled to see the surgeon who would do the operation of inserting the defibrillator to help my heart beat.

But before that, I had an appointment with Dr. T. at the Town Centre Clinic.

It was a miserable day, cold and icy. Even though it was noon, the skies were angry, cloudy and dark. Black ice covered Highway 99 from Emerald to the village center My mind was worried and filled with anxiety, but not because of the road conditions. My doctor would be giving me the results of the MUGA test that day.

I was coming up to the creek that runs through town and the bridge that covers it. The wait to see the doctor was driving me crazy, so I yelled out at the top of my voice, "Archangel Raphael, is my heart healed?"

In that precise moment, an opening appeared in the gloomy granite sky, and the most magnificent, fierce, golden light shone across the icy bridge. I felt like I was in the middle of a movie set with the most incredible special effects.

It was mind-blowingly beautiful!

I laughed out loud. I *knew* my heart was healed.

Dr. T. was waiting by the door when I arrived, and could tell from the look on my face that I already knew.

"Lynda. It's a miracle!" He grabbed me into a big warm hug.

Of *course* I was crying. We didn't really need words.

"So what will you do now?" he asked me.

"I will be grateful and move on with my life. I've been given a second chance; I respect that and will make a promise to live my life to it's fullest."

IS IT A MIRACLE?

To me, it's not important what it is or was; I'll take that kind of result any day.

The surgeon seemed annoyed, and said it was probably just the medications kicking in. Of course I agreed; you don't want to argue with science after all. *Yes*, I'm being facetious.

My cardiologist was amazed, but guarded of course. He reduced my medications slowly and I added some things to my regimen. I continued journaling and made changes to the way I interacted with people. I made a vow to *think* first and put a filter on my mouth. Reaction had always been my *modus operandi*. Words hurt and anger can be internalized. I made a vow to stay away from the things and the people in my life that upset me.

Life went on, and I realized I would never have a life with the man I loved. He told me his situation was terminal. He's a scientist and was *literally* working on his own cure, along with other medical professionals. I took my broken picket fence — the same one I thought I never wanted — and my wild, healthy heart and prepared to drive home to Mexico.

In May of 2009, I packed up my car, computer, books, photography equipment and my clothes. I planned to spend a month traveling, and I also wanted to take a few days in Seattle to say goodbye to my "no longer mine" cowboy. Afterwards, I planned to drive down through Utah to a writers' retreat in

Breckenridge, then spend a week in Sedona with my newly-made friends there, before heading home to Puerto Vallarta, Mexico.

You can be sure everyone told me I was crazy to risk the trip alone, though my doctors knew better than to try to dissuade me. That month-long road trip remains another highlight of my life.

It was also a journey of letting go. I met up with my friend and ex-lover and listened to all his *intellectual arguments* for my need to let him go, to move on with my life.

Although he fought his diagnosis, I never once heard him say he was going to live. If he'd asked me to hang around, I would have canceled all my plans and parked my cute little butt in Seattle. Somehow, *someway*, I would have found the means to make a living and stay by his side. But he never asked, so I left... though it was one of the hardest things I've ever had to do.

I continued to write a journal and write poetry. It all helped smooth out my emotional journey. My heart was heavy and sad, but healthy. I was mentally, if not emotionally, prepared for the next phase of my life.

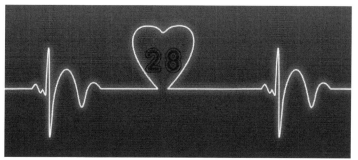

HEART CENTERED

My road trip that May of 2009 was a magical event filled with unicorn trees and heart-shaped red rocks, babbling brooks, and the drumming of Akal. I spent time in gratitude, peace, and joy. The sun shone as I walked, collecting rocks to take back to Mexico, but most of the time I pretty much just relaxed.

I made a vow to publish my first book of poetry when I returned home to Puerto Vallarta — *The Love Fix, One woman's journey in poetry and photographs* — and I did.

My week in Breckenridge was all about sisterhood and writing. I had the greatest fortune of meeting Linda Sivertsen — a writer who leads writing retreats in Carmel — who would become a great mentor and a dear friend of mine. Because of her, I began writing a memoir about my healing journey.

I dug into my past, dredging up all the hurts and failed marriages. As I wrote, I kept feeling that the timing wasn't right, that I wasn't meant to complete the memoir manuscript in 2009, *nor* in 2010. Maybe I wanted to make sure my "miracle" stuck.

It was a very special time for me in Breckenridge. I laughed, listened, and soon learned the meaning of "sisterhood." I also learned life doesn't have to be a solitary journey. I grew in my newfound knowledge and healing, and discovered the most important love I would ever receive, would be that which I give to myself.

For the next six months, I lived the life I promised myself. It was an extremely creative and joyous time. I wrote, published, and lived alone, without any relationship drama. And I worked on learning to love myself. I wrote things out, continued to take my reduced medications, and was incredibly grateful for the healthy flow of my heart.

When man plans, God laughs.

God must do an awful lot of laughing.

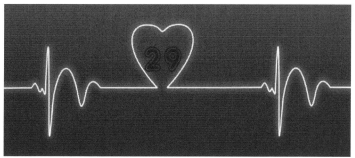

IRIDOLOGISTS AND OTHER Q'S

It's now more than six months since I returned to Mexico. I was wandering in Old Town, Puerto Vallarta one day and saw a shop selling natural products. The Mexican culture has a history rooted in all things natural and herbal. I wasn't looking for anything specific, but something pulled me into the shop.

I could hear a loud voice in the back of the store and looked up, expecting to see a TV program on a screen up on the wall. Nothing. I looked at the girl at the counter and asked her who was speaking.

"That's the iridologist."

"What's an iridologist?"

"He can look in your eyes, consult his chart, and diagnose you." The petite teenager, with tawny skin and black eyes, explained carefully in broken English.

Totally on intuition, I requested an appointment. I was told he would be available in twenty minutes, so I agreed to wait.

I have no idea why or what I expected, but after consulting his chart and taking notes, he told me I had heart problems. I smiled politely and suggested he check again, because I *had* heart problems, but was now healed. He shook his head and told me to see a cardiologist and to also begin taking CoQ-10 immediately. He explained CoQ-10 was a powerful heart-healing supplement.

I walked out of the store in a state of shock, and as soon as I could manage a single coherent thought, googled *Cardiologists Puerto Vallarta*. I then made an appointment for the very next day.

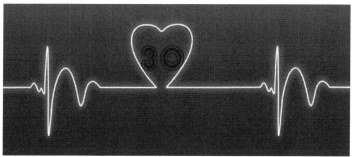

CARDIOLOGISTS SHOULDN'T LOOK LIKE MOVIE STARS

It's difficult to pay attention when your cardiologist is age-appropriate — well, not *that* much younger than me — and movie-star-hot, as in a George Clooney look-a-like. But this was serious stuff, so I needed to get it together and try to focus on my heart and what he was saying.

He took my history and wrote down the medications I was taking. He was curious about the CoQ-10 I was told to take by the iridologist — it was a new thing to him at the time — and asked me tons of other questions about my medical history. He was intrigued about my experience in Sedona, and not once did he seem surprised by my healing with Akal.

Then he handed me a gown and set up his equipment.

First, he did an EKG, then an echocardiogram. Twice... right there in his office! That's unheard of in Canada. He spent at least half an hour talking to me while he was doing it all — explaining what was happening, but not what he was seeing.

"Lynda, you said after the last MUGA your heart was at 68%, and before it was 28%?"

"Yes." It's difficult to talk when you're holding your breath.

"Well, I have some good news. Your heart is functioning at 42%. EF. That's better than when you were first diagnosed, but still not good enough. We need to get you over 55%. We're going to change your medications and start working to make you better. You're lucky you came to see me when you did."

I was shocked, but maybe not surprised. I still had a lot of emotional baggage to divest. Especially at that point in time, living once again back in Mexico, where I initially lived in 2002. I had stories to write, love lost and found and lost again, happiness and pain...

I admit it all came flooding back when I arrived home in Puerto Vallarta. I needed to get a grip on myself; it was time to start believing that the love of my life should be *me*. It was time to start living that.

"What do you think doctor?" I pleaded to hear the right words come from his sexy, Clooney lips.

"I too believe in miracles, Lynda, but science is my profession. So let's see how your body reacts to the change in medication. Take your pills and I'll see you in a month. If you have any shortness of breath, get to the hospital right away and call me."

He handed me a business card with his office and cell phone numbers.

I couldn't help be amazed at that. How often does a doctor give you their cellphone number in the US or Canada?

"See me in a month" is so much better than, "You need an operation." My heart was less than fully-healed, but not as bad as before. I can *live* with that!

I walked out sad and cautious, but optimistic. I've done it before, and I will prevail again. I'll call in the reinforcements and get this taken care of... STAT!

Archangel Raphael, where are you? We've got work to do!

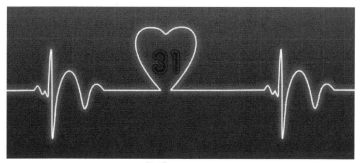

I BELIEVE

It was now 2010, and despite my setback, I was still alive. Six months had come and gone. My business affairs were in order, even though my affairs of the heart were in major disarray. My cowboy was out of my life completely. I was single again, but wasn't really wanting the whole dating or relationship thing anyway.

I did try internet dating briefly, before deciding I just wasn't ready yet, and met some interesting people... and some very *weird* people. I found MySpace, a place where like-minded creatives hang out. I wrote more poetry and published a second book called *Love Rehab*.

After a few false starts, I finally found the right company to work for and have built an excellent career for myself.

Dr. George Clooney — *I wish!* — was perfect for me. He was the right mix of caring, knowledge, and belief. He knew I had conviction and determination, and he took care of my heart. After a year of frustratingly slow progress, he declared me — *cautiously* — healed.

"It's a miracle," he said. "In all my years of practice, I've only ever seen one person heal from cardiomyopathy. Thank whatever Higher Power you believe in. And keep taking your medications... and whatever else you're doing. *It's working!*"

We went over everything new I'd added to my daily routine,

mostly vitamins. He was curious and open to hearing about anything he might be able to incorporate into his practice to help heal his other patients.

I made the You Tube videos starting in 2013. I wanted to be a light in the darkness for others who had been diagnosed with incurable diseases. I returned emails from loved ones who had family members who had lost hope about their diagnosis. Many found me.

One in particular I stay in touch with to this day. He believes his strong belief in God, and my words and healing ideas, are the reasons he's alive today. I had the same recommendations for him as I do everyone — do what your doctors tell you to do, and then do your part too.

I knew a four-minute video wouldn't be enough, but I suppose I was waiting to see that my healing was "good enough" to inspire others.

Then I woke up a few weeks ago — in 2017 — and said to myself, "What's wrong with you? If you can help someone else live even a month longer, or to have peace and love in their lives for six more months, a year, or *many* years... what are you waiting for?"

I thought back to the summer of 2015 when Dr. Wayne Dyer died. I was completely absorbed in building this high-pressure career, focused and always working. Even on vacation, my mind was designing better ways to teach and inspire my teams. I never really took the time to complete my healing story.

That summer, I released a fan fiction novella called *JET-Exposed* based on Jet creator NYT and USA Today bestselling author, Russell Blake. I'd been writing for so many years, and other than the poetry books — *The Love Fix, Love Rehab* and *I (Spy) Love* — I'd not published any of my own novels, *or* the story of my healing journey.

I've always been a fan of Dr. Dyer. He became a highly-respected world leader of the New Thought movement. I've been intrigued by spirituality and alternative thought all my life; it's a very big part of who I am.

When Dr. Dyer died suddenly of a heart attack at the age of seventy-two, the world was in shock. He'd been diagnosed with leukemia a few years before, but when he died, the medical profession discovered *he no longer had leukemia anywhere in his body*!

A week after his death, I was having a lovely deep sleep. Suddenly, a big voice woke me with the words,

"Are you ready yet?"

I remember sitting up in bed and laughing out loud. I knew it was him; I'd recognize his cheerful voice anywhere.

I continued publishing fiction that fall, and by the summer of 2016, I had three poetry books and five novellas to add to my name. I'd also dusted off a manuscript called *Target in the Sun* and published my first novel.

It's a scary process putting yourself out there. Will people hate it? Love it? Ridicule it? I knew how to tell stories and I loved writing them. But I wasn't ready to tell "The Big Story" — *my* story — yet.

I had one more novel to finish first. I published *Vanished in the Sun*, the second in the Carlos & Mia Series in January 2017. As I sent the book off to the editors, the words of Dr. Dyer came flooding back through my consciousness.

Are you ready yet?

So this is it, my friends, the little book of love I was afraid to write. It's 2017, the beat goes on, and my amazing beautiful heart is free of Idiopathic Dilated Cardiomyopathy.

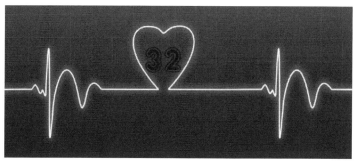

THE WORK

From The University of Sedona: A New Definition of the Meaning of Metaphysics

Traditionally, the word *Metaphysics* comes to us from Ancient Greece, where it was a combination of two words – *Meta*, meaning over and beyond – and *physics*. Thus, the combination means over and beyond physics. In the definition found in most dictionaries, Metaphysics is referred to as a branch of philosophy that deals with First Cause, and the Nature of Being. It is taught as a branch of philosophy in most academic universities under the label of "Speculative Philosophy."

In today's world, however, the word *Metaphysics* has become a description of many fields of interest. When one expresses an interest in Metaphysics, that interest may be in any one, or a combination of, the following subjects: Philosophy, Religion, Parapsychology, Mysticism, Yoga, ESP, Dreams, Jungian Psychology, Astrology, Meditation, Self-Help Studies, Positive Thinking, Life After Death, Reincarnation, etc.

The common denominator of these, and all similar subjects of course, deals with an exploration of reality. In the idealistic sense, it's how such knowledge may benefit human life on this earth, both individually and collectively.

So my question for you is... *Are you ready yet?*

Now I will break it down for you, and we can get to work!

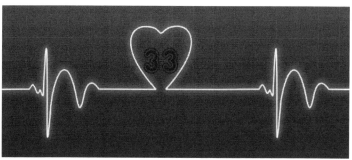

IT'S A MIND GAME

— Heart Habit 1: Denial —

Say it like it's a good thing. I admit I lived in denial. There. I've said it. I refused to accept that I could be dying—

Wait, I said that incorrectly. We are *all* dying. That's why we are *mortal* creatures with *immortal* souls, assuming you believe in that kind of thing.

Death. It's a matter of timing. I wasn't ready yet. I'm not sure why I felt I had a choice in the matter. Maybe things happened to me in that manner so I could experience the process, create a new mindset, and heal my heart on different levels.

The first part of my mind game was *denial.* I'm not saying, "Do what I did and you will live too." That's ridiculous and wrong. I have no idea of your illnesses, or prognosis. All I can do is answer the question that so many of you have asked me... "What did you do, Lynda?"

Denial was number one.

1. What exactly does *Denial* look like?

Once I made that decision in my mind, I let the diagnosis go completely. I never talked about it, except when it was an extremely important part of my healing process. I refused to be pulled into the "Poor Lynda" conversation so I could get the "She's so young" sympathy looks from people. I didn't want to be *that* person. I didn't want to be a middle-aged woman with a heart condition. I refused to wear my diagnosis.

After the initial shock, I stopped sharing. No one needed to know what was happening with me. Remember, we all have our stuff. We are all going through "things." No one needs to add to their own life's problems and challenges. Stop looking for sympathy. Every time you tell your story, you are *imprinting* illness, realigning with *dis-ease*, re-affirming to the universe that *this is who you are and who you want to be.*

I would like you to watch a video by Dr. Masaru Emoto. You may have heard of his experiments with music, words and water. There's a link in the addendum for many resources at the end of this book. His YouTube video is one of them.

I will summarize for you...

Dr. Emoto ran an experiment. He took individual vessels of water and played music, or spoke either negative or positive words to each one. For example, some positive words he used were "Love," "Thank You," and "Happiness." For the negative, one example is, "You make me sick, I'm going to kill you."

He then froze each receptacle of water. As the water froze, they formed crystallized shapes within them. The positive, beautiful words showed magnificent designs. The ugly, negative words created crystals that were unattractive blobs, misshapen and malformed. They were just horrible to look at.

The most beautiful of them all — to me — was the one named "Soul." In the middle of the "Soul" crystal, was a heart.

So once again, if you think you can, or you think you can't, you're *right*. The words you speak, and the thoughts you have, carry a vibration. If you talk about your "illness" or "dis-ease" all the time, you will not heal. If those are the thoughts racing through your mind, change your thought pattern *immediately*!

From a scientific point of view, if the body is made up of 50-75% water, wouldn't you agree that the words we speak, and the thoughts we have, could affect how that liquid flows throughout our bodies?

Do you still feel repeating the negative words of your story over and over again is helpful to your individual healing? The right answer is no.

2. Do *not* do your research on the internet.

The internet will have you surfing from site to site. Not good. Trust me, I made that mistake in the beginning myself and I still remember it.

In 2008, a top international site on cardiomyopathy, from the leading institute in Europe — I won't write the name here — said unequivocally, "Cardiomyopathy cannot be healed. At best, you might live five years from diagnosis."

Can you imagine the pain and utter hopelessness I felt reading those words? And they were *wrong*! It's been ten years (in 2017) and I'm still here. I don't know how such a prestigious organization can so callously take hope away from their five million followers!

So don't search the internet for information, it will only depress, scare, and misinform you. If you have a great specialist, (s)he will tell you what to do physically. If you *must* research, only ask your search questions in a positive way. For example, *what is a good heart-healthy diet to follow for a woman over sixty*? Or, *personal stories of healing from terminal illness*.

Remember, what you focus on, you get. Do you want to focus on *illness* or *wellness*? It's your decision. Give yourself the gift of positivity right now.

3. Refuse to learn the terminology.

Don't laugh — okay, maybe a smile is in order — but when the cardiologist said he was sorry, and I would have to have a defib... *whatever...* inserted, I didn't write it down or do any research, I didn't need to know. I'd already decided I wasn't going to do it. And to this day, if the defib... *thingy...* comes up in conversation, I have to look it up on spellcheck!

That doesn't mean you shouldn't do it or have the procedure done. That's for you and your medical professionals to determine. At that time, what I decided for me and my health, was *my* right action. You will know the right answer when you look inside your heart for what you need to do. *Do trust your intuition.* It will always lead you in the right direction.

4. Your biography becomes your biology.

I love that statement; I've heard it so many times. The first time, I stopped and thought about it.

Have you ever met someone who said he or she's a "survivor?" I have huge respect for all who survive anything, but *I* am *not my story*. I refuse to live in the shadow of the tough things in my life, whether it's rape, or an alcoholic parent, or abusive relationships. That is not *who I am*.

Why would I want to align my current self with these disastrous events that all happened in my past? It's like carrying a load of stones in a sack on my back. Or picture a vice around your heart that you tighten with each hurt or pain or abusive situation or disease that you have ever had in your life. Every time you think about it or say it out loud, you are tightening that vice.

How does it feel? Why would you ever choose to say "I'm a survivor?" We've all survived living through *something,* no matter our age or stage in life. Don't wear it. It's time to let the language and the label go... *now.*

If you <u>do not</u> want to heal yourself, continue to tell all who will listen how sick you are.

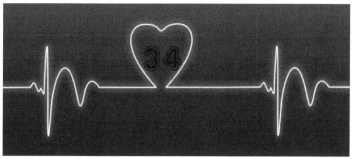

HEART MATES, SOUL BEATS

— Heart Habit 2: Focus - Fall in love with yourself and Life —

1. Write it out

I chose poetry, but if you read my poems, you will know anyone can write poetry! It might be just one line — *Some days my heart wants to be (status:) invisible to everyone.*

I kept a small notepad back then, but today I jot things down in my iPhone or iPad. Although lately, I find myself using paper journals again. I'd stumbled across a vintage — 2005 Andy Warhol Idea Book only half-used. It made my day.

As a thought comes to mind, I write it out. If it's sad and I'm using my iPad, I can write it down and send it off to cyberspace, never to think of again. It's easy to do and very effective to your healing.

You can keep a journal or write a novel. As I've mentioned before, I published five novellas and two novels in the last year and a half. It's fun! Do something *fun* with your mind. Focus on now and the future with creativity in your heart. Let go of pain and worry in whatever way serves you best.

2. Forgive Yourself

Yes. That's correct. You know we all beat ourselves up for

that *one* thing…

Maybe it's your weight, your smoking, a divorce… or a falling out with a family member. Maybe you never got to say goodbye to your mother — like I did. Or never allowed yourself to forgive your father — like I did. It's time to move on from all that negative thinking about yourself.

Make a list of your regrets and — one by one — say, "I forgive myself."

3. Become Creative

The first time I met a Rothko at the Metropolitan Museum of Art, I wanted to paint.

My son was visiting me in Mexico one Christmas, and he knew how much I wanted to paint. So we went to the art store, where we purchased acrylic paint, an assortment of brushes, and an easel. We quickly went back to my place and I started painting.

For two years, I painted *furiously*. I covered all my walls with unique work that meant something to me, but had no particular style. Two paintings came from an interpretation of my photographs, another came from a photo sent to me from a friend in Africa. One canvas began with a soft baby-blue color all over it, which reminded me of a swimming pool, so I found a photo online of the back of a woman sitting on the edge of a pool and copied the idea on my canvas with paint. It was that easy.

The most difficult part is not to *judge* yourself. There will never be another exactly the way you've done yours, no matter what your creative project may be.

After those two years, I was done. I put my acrylics away in a cupboard and have yet to start painting again. And that's okay! It doesn't matter. I expressed something and allowed myself to get lost in my work for hours at a time. And that's time spent focusing on creation and creativity vs. self-pity and dying.

4. Find a passion; anyone can take beautiful photographs today.

You don't need to be a photographer, but be obsessed with *something* healthy and positive. It could be something as simple as sunrises, as it is for me — although for a long time it was sunsets.

This morning, I decided to take a walk along the beach with my coffee and a scone from the local bakery. I took photos of fuchsia and soft pink buganvilla (Spanish name for what's known in America as bougainvillea), cobblestone walkways and caramel-colored sand. I stopped and watched two Mexican senoritas set up a tent and put out a sign for massages on the beach.

When I got back home, I posted my photos on Facebook. You can start an Instagram or Pinterest account and publish from your phone to the site. Maybe your passion is food, or fashion, or making clothing, or reading... It doesn't matter. Just get passionate about life and living, and share it to make others smile.

5. Start a blog about *life*.

Do it for your family, do it for your grandkids. Upload photos and places you want to see, have seen, or will see. Let's call it "Getting a Future." Set up Facebook. You can make it all about your interests, whatever they may be. I spent an hour on chat last night with my sister, who's obsessed with our ancestry. It's been a curiosity for her all her life.

Get excited about *something*. It makes living worthwhile.

6. Dance, Exercise — Just move it!

I admit, exercise has never been my favorite thing either, but I dance, meditate, stretch, walk... Basically, I do something to be active every single day, and you should too.

Maybe you want to ride a bike. It's best to find something active that doesn't feel like exercise. Make it fun and combine it with something that interests you.

When I was in the fashion business, I could go through a shopping center, in and out of every ladies-wear store, in four hours — without a break. That's great walking exercise, but it could be an expensive form of exercise.

My mother took swimming lessons after she turned sixty! It might even have been closer to sixty-five when she retired from her government job in Ottawa.

Whatever you choose... move. Take action; be active.

If you want something you've never had, you need to do something you've never done.

Your body will thank you and your heart will get stronger. And don't forget to drink water. I keep a water bottle beside me all the time.

7. Become the *new* and *improved* you!

Create something. Throw parties. Take cooking classes. Learn a language. Become a fitness freak. Travel. And give back by volunteering and helping others. There's always someone who needs our help or compassion.

Find your passion.

Train your mind to focus on fun.

Do something (again, something healthy and positive) you've never done before.

You're not dead yet!

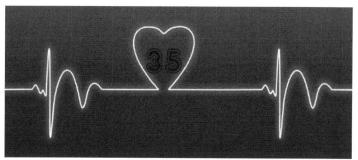

THE LIFE YOU WERE BORN TO LIVE

— Heart Habit 3: Visioning - Find that imagination you had when you were a child —

There are so many excellent books and videos out there that will help you with this. I will give you a list at the end of this book of several influencing materials I used on my own journey if you'd like to use them as well.

Don't be patient with yourself. All it takes is an *instant.* In that instant, you can make the mind-shift that will help you on your healing journey, and might even save your life.

When it comes to philosophies, we're all saying the same things. Master teachers have healed from incredible mental and physical pain. Some have even died and come back to share a different vision of what life can be. Some spend their lives teaching others how to heal, how to go back in their lives and find that *one thing* or series of things that created their *dis-ease.* If you follow your intuition, as you did when you picked up my book, you will find the answers you're looking for.

I ask of you only one thing... be open to the *magic* that will take place in your life. It will certainly make the rest of your journey on this plain more fulfilling and more loving.

1. Change your mind.

Make a decision that miracles *do* exist.

The shift in thinking first happens in your own mind. No one can force you. Stop right now with negative thoughts and vibrations. Stop thinking about everything that *is* wrong, or *can go* wrong. Let go of your story, your biography, right now!

A fun way to do this is a Gratitude Jar. Take any kind of vessel you'd like. Label it. Throughout each day, or once a day, or maybe that moment during the day when you feel the most vulnerable, write down everything you're grateful for. It might be something that happened during that particular day.

For example, today I had to get a new drivers license in Mexico...

First, I went to the wrong location — easy enough to do here, as the offices move around a lot in growing areas. When I finally got to the right place, I didn't know what to do! A kind woman came up behind me and asked me what I needed. She wasn't an employee, but she pointed me in the right direction.

Then a gentleman, who spoke perfect English and had his own paperwork clutched in one hand, took my forms and walked over to a young lady, who then made copies for us. He explained to me he had several family members who worked in that very office, so we could get it all done fast!

And he was right! I was in and out in record time.

I'm grateful for love and kindness wherever I receive it.

2. Create a new belief

I have my own personal *belief* that all people are good. Call me naive if you like, but that's my *belief*, and I'm keeping it.

A couple of summers ago, I was in a busy grocery store near my home, here in Mexico. I was particularly distracted that summer, though I don't remember why. Beside this grocery store, are several bank machines lined up in a row. I approached one and inserted my debit card, tapped in the numbers to withdraw 4000 pesos, and withdrew my card.

I had my earbuds in, my iPhone playing my favorite tunes, and I walked away from the machine. I thought I heard a commotion behind me so I stopped, turned around, and witnessed a bunch of smiling faces and a young man chasing me, waving 4000 pesos in the air.

Can you imagine! I'd taken my card, but left the cash sitting in the machine. In another person's world, that money would probably be gone — stolen faster than a person can blink. But I believe in the goodness of people, and the universe continues to show me I'm right.

If you don't want to, or can't believe in yourself and the world around you, nothing in your life will change. But if you got this far in my story, I know you're ready. I know you want a better quality of life. There are no guarantees in life or about life. But I know this one thing... life is so much more fun if we fill it with belief in the goodness of our fellow man, and live with love and hope.

Do you remember your childhood books? *The Little Engine That Could* by Watty Piper — "I think I can, I think I can."

Be that little engine. *Believe* you can change, no matter what everyone around you is saying.

3. Vision Boards

Here's how I create a vision board.

First, I write down the things I want in my life. Most people will cut pictures out of magazines that represent their "vision" of their lives, then paste them onto a large piece of construction paper. My vision board is created online using Canva, which is a creative book cover and banner-maker (link is provided at the end of this book). *Where* you make it, makes no difference.

In my case, I went online and downloaded photos from Canstock, a pay-per-photo service, and using a Canva layout, I added the pics I'd chosen until I created my vision of the life I saw for myself.

I don't care what age you are, or what stage of life or health you're in, *visualizing is critical*.

Maybe you can't walk properly right now, so you find a photo of someone walking along the beach or running a marathon. Maybe you want to write a bestseller, or travel to the Vatican. Maybe you want a mate to share your journey, or you want to live long enough to be around to attend a grandchild's graduation, or your own graduation.

I'll share my Vision Board with you.

Mine has a picture of a couple on it, a home in the Pacific Northwest, right on the ocean — And yes, you're right, my cowboy hasn't given up searching for his miracle. The couple is us; the home is ours.

I also have a beach casita (small house) cantilevered over the most gorgeous turquoise waters in the Maldives, and a picture of the Eiffel Tower — my son, daughter-in-law and grandbaby live in Paris.

I've added in a photographer, paints and brushes, a photograph with *Bestseller* written on it, and the healing stones of Sedona to remind me I want to study with the shamans, do more spiritual training, and learn about lucid dreaming with Robert Moss.

Visuals my friends, we all need visuals. Be precise. Have fun with it. It's your life, you get to design it any way you want.

Should you look at it every day? I think you should. It will inspire you to work out, eat well, be mindful, and have dreams and goals. I put a vision page on my Mac as a screensaver. Today it's a collage of the cover of this book, with Oprah holding it and smiling! For yours, you might put it on your Kindle or iPad or phone, or if it's physical, on your fridge, bookshelves, or a mirror.

4. Know your *what*

Remember, ours is not the *how,* ours is only the *what*. We don't have to know how everything will play out, we only need to know *what* we want.

There are many great teachers of New Thought today, and I suggest you find one you enjoy listening to. I credit Jacob Glass for helping me keep my head on straight. I tithe to him monthly, and once a week, I receive a blunt and perceptive audio download from his weekly lectures in Los Angeles. I've been listening to him for the last five years. He's my guru. When I first heard his voice, I said to myself, "I can't stand this guy!"

Find a guru that has a message you don't agree with.

Admit it, you never expected that piece of advice. What do I mean by that? Let me share...

One day, a few girlfriends said they were having a women's night at a friends' condo. I've never been a 'hanging out with the girlfriends' kind of girl. I'm a loner. A fun night for me is good food, a great movie, and then going to sleep with Gabriel Allon! (Look him up, he's famous!)

My friends organized a facilitator, Faith Holland, who would guide our women's group over the next ten weeks. I thought I'd go once to placate everyone, then bow out. I'd never met Faith and I had no idea why I was going. I only knew that my intuition was guiding me to go — against my will.

Faith started the meeting off by announcing we were in a safe place and we were all there for a reason. So we went from person to person, and when she got to me, she said, "Why are you here?"

I had nothing to say... or so I thought.

The next thing I knew, these words came tumbling out, "I want to know why there is death all around me."

I was so shocked; I had no idea that would come out of my mouth. I did have an ex-boyfriend who was dying, and another good friend, a Navy SEAL, who had died the month before, and I'd been diagnosed at one point, with no possibility of healing. *Why were the people I loved dying?*

I remind myself as I'm telling you... you don't have to know the *how* you are going to heal, you only need to know your *what*. My *what* was I wanted the pain of loss of love to stop. I wanted healing, not only inside my *physical* heart — I seemed to have that under control — but in my *emotional* heart as well.

I continued to resist the group every week. I'd come up with excuses not to go, but I showed up just the same. Faith worked with some of the principles of *A Course In Miracles* — you can look that up if you're not familiar — and she introduced me to the teachings — or should I say, *the ravings* — of Jacob Glass.

If your spiritual teacher makes you crazy, you can't stand to listen to his voice, and you don't like half the things he's saying, that's the *right one* for you. If you are in resistance, it's a sign that this is an area of your thinking you need to clean up. Yes, I could write a book on that!

So sometimes, the very things we resist, are the ones we need to work on in order to heal. If you're shaking your head at my ramblings right now, that probably means you need to start this book all over again — or not. It's your choice.

5. Can you feel it?

What is your dream?

I'm a big believer in envisioning, as you've most likely

already figured out. One of my visions is how I will live the last years of my life.

I imagine myself in my later years — I'm in my eighties, or maybe my nineties — walking along a beach called Destilideras on the stunning West Coast Bay of Banderas. My feet are wandering in and out of the dramatic surf, and I'm loving the baby powder-soft sand between my tanned and pink-polished toes. With me are several Mexican preteens, and my grandson Félix. We're all laughing and enjoying our conversations, which are a mixture of Spanish, English and French.

The Mexican kids ask me about a world they've not yet visited, and I tell them about the snow in the Rocky Mountains of Canada, the Louvre in Paris and the gondolas in Venice. I tell them if they have *belief* in themselves, they can create a *vision* of how they want their lives to be.

Later, still in my future vision, I return to my villa. My housekeeper has prepared a healthy lunch of a chili mango salad, made with fresh local produce, and grilled snapper with garlic and butter.

I'll probably still have a bad habit of drinking Diet Coke, but will save a glass of wine for the sunset after Félix has finished surfing. I will spend most of the afternoon working on my newest manuscript — more than likely, another steamy novel about romance in Mexico.

And, as always, I will be so very grateful for the life I was born to live.

TALK TO YOUR HEART

— Heart Habit 4: Talk to yourself. Out loud? Sometimes —

1. Listen to your heartbeat

I found a YouTube video of an athlete who put a monitor on his heart when he worked out. It was fascinating to listen to this man's healthy heart beating. I listened to it every day. And I talked to my own heart.

"Dear heart, this is what we sound like when we're healthy. When we are pumping at full capacity, we will beat like this. Let's listen to the beat together." I'd lie in bed first thing in the morning or last thing at night, or whenever the urge came over me, and we'd listen.

Weird, right? I don't think I ever told anyone about that. As I sit here now, filled with absolute joy for these amazing years, I'm asking the universe to remind me of everything I did so I can share with you every single thing that made a difference in my health.

If you have a blood disease you might visualize donating clean, healthy blood to the Red Cross. If you have a problem with your kidneys, imagine giving a healthy kidney to a complete stranger in gratitude for your healing. If you're stressed or in emotional pain, imagine wellness and counseling another through his or her own trauma.

Can you feel it?

2. Do that thing you don't want to do

I saved this because it's so important. Free yourself from the things that are hurting your heart. Think of your body as a Property Brothers project. Your body is an old house, or maybe even a young house, slapped together with faulty glue. For some of us, we may have painted over the old paint, or wallpapered over moldy Gyprock. We might have used steel wool on an old piece of furniture, never completely removing the old finish, then washed it with a new color. We might have placed new flooring over a water-stained sub-floor, without first fixing the reason it was damaged to begin with. In our renovation project, we might have left decades old windows, because they were "good enough for now"…until they weren't.

So this is your body; this is your soul.

I'm not a psychiatrist, and I have absolutely no degrees to back up my thinking, but I do have multiple PhD's in living and loving and making mistakes, and also healing myself.

We need to pull that garbage out and let it go, tear everything out down to the studs and rebuild. But... *how*?

Round up those old hidden mementos. Don't say you don't have any! I know you have them. We all do. We pull them out when we want to feel sorry for ourselves. If they're only in your mind, start writing those memories down on a sheet of paper. Go back as far as you want. If it's a *big thing*, the one that you use every time you have that ice cream-and-potato chip pity-party, it deserves its own special sheet of paper!

Every single, ugly, *awful* hurt that you dwell on when you are lonely and scared, that's what you will be working with. We need to empty our hearts and souls of hurt in order to make room for loving ourselves. We are going to *burn* that shit and let it all go. And we're doing it right now.

I'm *not* a believer in going into the past, so we do this once, and only once. I don't believe in lingering, looking for reasons why I am the way I am, or how I got into this emotional state. I don't care. Remember, it's not about the *how,* it's about *what we are going to do to do to fix it.*

You will also need to cleanse yourself and your home with sage.

Next, throw love at it. What does that mean, you ask?

Every time a thought comes into my mind that is negative and hurtful to me, I zap it with *love*. Every person who hurt me, I zap him or her with love. Love is a powerful force that cannot be broken. It's my superpower, and yours too, should you accept the challenge. No matter what happens or who hurts you, say to yourself in your mind or out loud, "I love you."

Why is that so powerful? Because in loving another, you are giving love to yourself. It's that simple. Let the hurts go, one by one. The one's we resist the most, are the ones that are causing our bodies the most pain, the most *dis-ease*.

Remember... *hurt is toxic*. Imagine hurt, hate, grudges, inability to forgive, anger, inability to let go — imagine all that as thick toxic waste pumping through your heart.

How can your heart and soul possibly operate at peak state when it's so clogged with emotional excrement?

Clean it up. You can do it, if you want to badly enough.

3. The "F" Word.

You knew it was coming again, didn't you?

Let's go back to the old house. When we renovate, we tear down walls. We punch out entrances. We clean up messes, and turn up our noses at nasty smells. We shake our heads in wonder at how long this rotting floor has been here. And look at that wiring! Amazing they haven't had a fire. And those rusty pipes, the homeowners were lucky they didn't have a flood.

If your body were your home, wouldn't you think a good clean up/renovation, or even a complete tear-down might be in order? Let's assume for a moment that the physical body is an outward representation of the mind and the emotional heart. If that's the case — and you know what I'm saying is true — how do we go about that renovation?

Well, for some of us, new parts are in order. We determine this with the help of qualified professionals. I will never take anything away from the doctors. If it makes you more comfortable, take my words and use my advice when all else fails. I'm good with that. But it's better to think of it all as a joint project, a partnership in your healing.

Back to the "F" word, where it all begins. *Forgiveness*.

Write down *that* list, if you're a list person, and include the name of every person who's hurt you, denied you, fired you, or not loved you enough. Then, one by one, *forgive* them.

I know it's not easy. You've been living with that story for so many years. You've allowed these hurts to build up inside you, layer upon layer of pain and misery.

Are you beginning to see where I'm going here? We've all got the story, the one we tell ourselves about our past. It might be abuse, or neglect, or abandonment. You know your story well. It's been your *excuse* for the way you are, the fact that you cannot have good health or a good relationship. It's your story. I believe, *in only one second,* we can become aware of what we've been doing and zap it. Stop it right now.

It's your choice; it's your decision. There is nothing about your story of past grievances that can serve your body or mind today. You already know this. That's a major part of why you have *dis-ease.* And it's a major part of healing.

The most important forgiveness is toward your self. That finger you point in accusation at someone else? Remember... one finger may point to them, but the other three point right back to you. No one is perfect; we've all made our own mistakes.

Give yourself a break. Everyone has regrets, things they wished they'd done differently. We all have them. We talked about this before, but I'm saying it again... write them down, and throw that love inward, at your self. You deserve it. Forgive yourself. Love yourself unconditionally.

Are we there yet, or are you still rolling your eyes in major resistance?

But *what if...* I'm right?

What if nothing else happens for you except you feel a shift, a huge weight lifting off your heart? Would that be so terrible?

Weight lifted off your heart...

How much weight do you think is pressing down on your heart right now? Maybe that little heart can start to function better when you allow it its freedom.

So what if... *I'm right?*

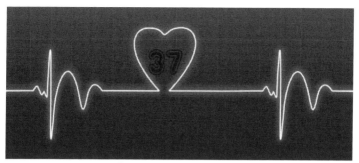

NEW BEGINNINGS

— Calling the Soul Back Home —

It's my story. It's my belief.

Ever since my first time in Sedona, the beginning of November in 2008, I've been curious about what Akal actually did. I know when I walked up that hill to the red rock crest on Airport Vortex, I was cold, wet, and weak. But when I came down, I *knew I was better.*

I read a lot. I probably have over eight hundred books in my iPad, maybe more. Amazon is my best friend. I don't go anywhere without a book. I never have. The two books that Akal suggested I buy in 2008 I now have as e-books.

One of the books I find easy to read is Robert Moss' book *The Three "Only" Things: Tapping the power of Dreams, Coincidence & Imagination*. As I mentioned before, working with Robert Moss is something I have on my Vision Board. He provides training in various places around the world, and I would be honored to study beside that man.

Amazing books can change your life. You will read them over and over again. Each time you read a passage in the book, you'll find new 'ah ha' moments. I underline like crazy, and still find new things that I missed when I read the book before. The message or explanation might not have been right for me at that time. I wasn't *ready yet.*

Robert Moss' message is simple, yet powerful —

"When we claim the power of the Three Only Things, we connect with extraordinary sources of direction, healing and energy. We also become citizens of two worlds. In every day circumstances, caught up in hurry and stress and other people's schedules and expectations, we often lose touch with the deeper meaning of life. We become entangled in problems that cannot be solved on the level of thinking and being that we are on. We become strangers to *magic*, which is the art of reaching into a deeper reality and bringing gifts from it into the ordinary world."

I am simply the vessel. The words I write flow through me to you. This world of magic, of which Robert Moss speaks, may not be something that you're ready for. That's okay. But if you are, then through his wonderful book you will discover there is an entire new world beyond the obvious one, where we have the opportunity to experience things that at first may make no sense to you. But with time, in your dreams and imagination, you may find health and healing and a life that only you will understand.

Robert Moss leads groups in active dreaming. In our dreams, we can access imagination and awaken our individual powers within.

I like to keep a notepad by my bed. If I'm concerned about something, I set an *intention* before I go to sleep that I may find clarity in my dreams. When I wake, I write down key words, phrases, and things I saw.

Sometimes a dream may appear to be obvious, but it might not mean what you *think* it does. Dream analysis can be great fun and can lead to many intuitive answers for what's going on in your life.

Think of using these guidelines like you'd use a GPS. You set your destination, your *intention,* or your *what,* before you put your foot on the gas. You don't question *how* you will get there, you only *trust* that you *will*.

Would you get in your vehicle and start to drive with no idea of where you're going? Unlikely. We first visualize our destination, and healing is the same thing. Whether you design your vision board, write a daily list, or set an intention for your dream, it's all the same thing. We are imagining the final result. Why wouldn't we do the same with our healing?

When Akal sat on the red rock with the twisted Juniper bushes surrounding us, he called in our ancestors and asked that they retrieve the lost parts of my soul.

I had no idea at the time why he was drumming or what it meant. I only knew one thing... I was desperate and sick and I *didn't want to die*. It made perfect sense to me that all the emotional pain I'd internalized, had somehow *broken my heart* and diminished the light of my soul.

I've read many books and stories since then about shamans and what they do. They honor their connection with Mother Earth and the Spirit World. All cultures have their mystic healers and shamans. I was blessed to find Akal, who could feel my pain and help me on my healing journey.

I have no idea why I decided to leave Mexico in November of 2007, how the perfect career opportunity lined up in my life, how I packed and got on the road within a week, how I found the perfect tenant for my condo, how I drove the dramatic coast of California and Oregon...and didn't die from a heart attack along the way.

This is what I *do* know... I have guardian angels, there is a Higher Power, and it was not my time to die. And if you are reading my little journal of love, it might not be your time either.

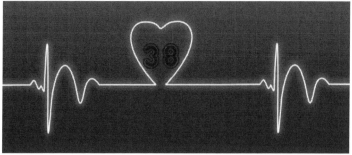

FÉLIX

I became a grandmother this year. My darling Félix is a miracle baby. His mother waited forty-four years to carry this little man, and I am so grateful that she chose *my* son to be her husband and her son's father.

Félix and I have a special connection. When his mother told me his due date would be anywhere from the middle to the end of August 2016, I started to prepare for a trip to Paris, France where my son and daughter-in-law live.

I wasn't able to be away longer than a month, so I had to choose the date carefully. I wanted to be there to hold him as soon as possible after he was born, and to help my son and his wife get through those first weeks. Because he was in-vitro, and due to many other complications — my daughter-in-law's age being one risk factor — they had no idea if she would go full-term or not.

So using my gut-feeling and lots of faith, I booked my date of arrival for the twenty-seventh of July.

As the due date grew closer, the doctors said she was doing so well, they expected she would go full-term, which would be the third week of August. If that happened, I might miss the whole thing!

So little unborn Félix and I had a conversation — telepathically, of course. "Grand-mère is coming on July twenty-seventh. I need you to be healthy and ready to be born right away so I can be with you the whole time I'm there." I know it was selfish, but I *did* mention he was to be born healthy!

I arrived the morning of July twenty-seventh, and my daughter-in-law was at her doctor appointment. It was a Wednesday, and yes, all was well with both mom and baby, but her doctor thought a C-section would be safest for several reasons, and they scheduled it for that Friday.

My daughter-in-law was tired, her back hurt, and she felt like she hadn't slept for four months. Her doctor felt it was more of a risk to wait any longer, and since the baby was doing well and fully developed, why wait and tempt fate?

I went to sleep that night and woke to a text message from my son saying her water had broke, and I needed to get in a taxi and head to the hospital... *now*!

I smiled to myself and thought, *Of* course *her water broke, Félix knew his grand-mère was here!*

I still remember passing the Arc du Triomphe and the Eiffel Tower and the architecturally magnificent structures from centuries past. I felt I was in the middle of a movie set. How glorious to have my grandson born in such a historic and culturally magnificent city!

I arrived with an hour to spare. Félix was born healthy, strong, and beautiful. I held him in my arms just three hours after he was born.

Yes, Félix and I have a special bond. I spoke to him in my heart, long before he was conceived. When I visualized my life, I didn't want to die before I held my first grandchild. It is my dream that Félix will grow up in a world with peace, tolerance, and love.

When I look into his smiling eyes, I see innocence, and my heart is filled with pure love. It is for Félix that I finally said, "Yes, Dr. Dyer. I'm ready to write my story now.

And the beat goes on...

Books

I Can See Clearly Now by Dr. Wayne W. Dyer — *This is his autobiography. I loved it because it's his journey, his growth; and references all his books. Here's his Amazon site, including audio & Kindle*

https://www.amazon.com/Wayne-W.-Dyer/e/B000AQ104Y/ref=ntt_dp_epwbk_0

The Three Only Things by Robert Moss

https://www.amazon.com/Robert-Moss/e/B000AQW534/ref=ntt_dp_epwbk_0

You Can Heal Your Life by Louise L. Hay

https://www.amazon.com/Louise-L.-Hay/e/B000APL6J4/ref=ntt_aut_sim_1_1

Matrix Energetics: The Science and Art of Transformation by Richard Bartlett

https://www.amazon.com/Richard-Bartlett/e/B001JS0UNO/ref=ntt_dp_epwbk_0

Websites

https://www.youtube.com/watch?v=Xo171XzJaOY

Akal Chant - The Soul Undying

Mantra Music - Ong Namo by Snatam Kaur

Ong Namo - I bow to the subtle divine wisdom

Guru Dev Namo - I bow to the divine teacher within

My idea of exercise, stretching, dancing…
This will speak to your soul, if you allow it…
https://youtu.be/SRGVCw0Wc3w

Dream Moods
http://www.dreemmoods.com/dreamdictionary/

The Magic of Water, Dr. Masaru Emoto
https://www.youtube.com/watch?v=tAvzsjcBtx8

Reiki Hand Positions and Self Treatment, William Rand
https://youtu.be/W5HeyMeC468

Learn Reiki in 10 Minutes - *A good overview of the Healing Modality*
https://youtu.be/0DDw0BrIXrk

Shamanic Sound Healing Chimes Chants with Akal in Sedona AZ - *This is the healer I worked with in 2008*)
https://youtu.be/ZEkeNjhWqGY

Jacob Glass speaking at Vision - *This is that guy, yes, the guy I tithe to monthly for his lectures.*
https://youtu.be/atiWQ7yDyWk

The Work, Byron Katie - *This is great!*
https://youtu.be/O60DfNd4k_Y

Canva (*free design website for graphics, great for a vision board*)
https://www.canva.com

The Oracle, Whistler BC
https://www.facebook.com/OracleEmporium/

Lynda Filler Author
https://www.amazon.com/Lynda-Filler/e/B00JNP2CS6

Fiction Novellas, Novels and Poetry
Praise for Lynda Filler's Poetry
"*Beautiful. You left me dazed and speechless.*" **Raven**

"There's not a soul in the world that can't feel this. I love it. I feel it." **Mia**

"This is so full of love, there are no words." **Flame in the Snow**

The Love Fix

https://goo.gl/JrTgwY

Love Rehab

https://goo.gl/QNIH6w

I (Spy) Love

https://goo.gl/ZeLuXi

Sleepless

from *The Love Fix*

I lie
and lay too
but mostly
I lie — to myself
sleepless
in denial
about
you

meds interact it says
they conflict/invite/incite
all sorts of actions/reactions
they just plain make me sick

and while, yes, all the while, I am busy with
burn/heart-burn
like the one you left me
when you interacted/convicted/deleted
me from your life

sometimes
I can actually forget you
when I sleep

Printed in Great Britain
by Amazon